P9-BYQ-656

THE CREEPIEST CREATURES FROM
CLASSIC LITERATURE

THE BIG BOOK OF
MONSTERS

BY
HAL JOHNSON

ILLUSTRATED BY
TIM SIEVERT

WORKMAN PUBLISHING
NEW YORK

To my own little monster, the Great Khan.
—HJ

To the monsters in my life:
Elizabeth, Buddy, Herman, and Ms. Kitten.
—TS

Copyright © 2019 by Workman Publishing Co., Inc.

All rights reserved. No portion of this book may be reproduced—mechanically, electronically, or by any other means, including photocopying—without written permission of the publisher. Published simultaneously in Canada by Thomas Allen & Son Limited.

Library of Congress Cataloging-in-Publication Data is available.

ISBN 978-1-5235-0711-5

Cover illustration by Tim Sievert
Cover Design by Sara Corbett
Book Design by Maria Elias

Workman books are available at special discounts when purchased in bulk for premiums and sales promotions as well as for fund-raising or educational use. Special editions or book excerpts can also be created to specification. For details, contact the Special Sales Director at the address below, or send an email to specialmarkets@workman.com.

Workman Publishing Co., Inc.
225 Varick Street
New York, NY 10014-4381
workman.com

WORKMAN is a registered trademark of Workman Publishing Co., Inc.

Printed in China
First printing July 2019

10 9 8 7 6 5 4 3 2 1

CONTENTS

HERE THERE BE MONSTERS
A NOTE FROM THE EDITOR

Since the beginning of time, humans have given shape to their fears by telling stories of things that go bump in the night. Some of these stories have been passed down orally from one generation to the next and never written down. Others have made their way onto clay tablets, parchments, and into books.

In fact, some of the earliest written stories feature sun-swallowing serpents and fire-breathing beasts. Later, during medieval times and the Renaissance, poems and plays told tales of poison-spouting dragons and wicked witches. Then came the age of Gothic literature, when readers met those dreadful fiends, Dracula and Frankenstein's monster.

Here, you'll find retellings of twenty-five of the most spine-tingling monster stories from throughout history—stories you can look up and read yourself, if you dare.

In each chapter, you'll see passages in quotations. These come directly from the source text or an English-language translation. Every chapter also offers a glimpse beyond the book, where you'll learn what inspired the authors to write these tales of dread. For example, William Shakespeare wrote *Macbeth* at a time when many people in England believed that witchcraft was a real threat—so it's no surprise that his play features three devious witches! A couple of centuries later, when advances in science were rocking the world and people feared the dangers of scientific experimentation, Mary Shelley wrote *Frankenstein*, that classic tale of science-gone-wrong.

As the world changes, some fears are put to rest, but new ones always arise. And as long as there is something to fear, there will be monsters.

A final word of caution before you turn the page:
Be careful, and trust no one. Sometimes even the friendliest face can hide a monster. (I'm looking at you, Dorian Gray.)

ĀPEP

FROM

THE BOOK OF THE DEAD

(CA. 16TH CENTURY BC)

Deep in the ancient Egyptian underworld of Tuat lurked the giant serpent Āpep. Some said Āpep had twelve human faces emerging from his back. Others said he had legs. Everyone agreed he was up to no good.

Like most underworlds, Tuat was the home of the dead, but it was also quite literally under the world. Every day, the great god Ra carried the sun across the sky in his celestial barge, only to descend in the west come evening and pass into Tuat.

And there Āpep lay in wait.

Āpep hated Ra. Every night he plotted against the god, and every morning he "lay hidden under the place of sunrise," waiting to spring upon the

CATEGORY: Demigod

BASE OF OPERATIONS: Tuat

WHEN: Every night

POWERS: Recovering from daily dismemberment

MOST DASTARDLY DEED: Attempted sun swallowing

FEAR FACTOR: 💀💀💀💀

celestial barge and "swallow up the sun as he [Ra] was about to rise in the eastern sky."

Āpep was not alone, for he was "accompanied by legions of devils and fiends, red and black, and by all the powers of storm, tempest, hurricane, whirlwind, thunder, and lightning."

But neither was Ra alone. On his barge rode other gods known as the Children of Horus. They carried chains and they carried scepters and, above all, they carried fetters. This was going to be a fight.

Even with the Children of Horus on his side, Ra might not have been able to overcome Āpep and his monstrous army. But Ra had a secret weapon. The ibis-headed god Thoth, wisest of all beings mortal or divine, had taught Ra a magic spell that could "paralyze all Āpep's limbs." As Ra recited the sacred words, his loyal followers throughout Egypt chanted along with him, adding the strength of their magic to Ra's own.

CUTTING UP SNAKES

The myth of the battle between Ra and Āpep is related to a myth that appears in many cultures across the globe to explain the creation of all things: a powerful god fights a water serpent, a dragon, or a giant at the beginning of time. The god pins down the monster, cuts it up, and creates the world from its body parts. In these myths, the creation of the earth is the triumph of order over chaos, with chaos often symbolized by a serpent.

And then things got violent.

First, Ra "shot his fiery darts" at Āpep. Then the Children of Horus "hacked the monster's body to pieces, which shriveled up under the burning heat of the rays of the sun." Just to be safe, they "fastened chains upon him" and "fettered him with fetters." Then "all the devils and fiends of darkness fled shrieking in terror at their leader's fate." Safely, the sun rose out of Tuat and passed into the world above, and it was dawn in Egypt.

And this happened *every single morning*. Every daybreak was a fight to the death.

Perhaps it still is.

If Āpep ever wins, it will be eternal night, and every morning he tries, and every morning he fails. And although he is chained up and dismembered, over the course of the day, "the reptile breaketh asunder the fetters" (bursts his chains) and gets ready to try again the next night.

Once again he is hiding by the gates of dawn. Once again his legion of demons are waiting with him.

Every single morning.

BEYOND THE BOOK

A COFFIN OR A BOOK?

The ancient Egyptians never wrote a book called the *Book of the Dead*. In the early nineteenth century, "pioneer Egyptologists" gave the name to scrolls of papyrus found in Egyptian tombs.

As scholars got better at reading hieroglyphics, they realized that this so-called *Book of the Dead*, which contained "spells and incantations, hymns and litanies, magical formulae and names, words of power and prayers," could be found not only in coffins, but also *on* coffins, painted around the sides, or "cut or painted on walls of pyramids and tombs."

Many of these texts were first translated into English by E. A. Wallis Budge, "keeper of the Egyptian and Assyrian antiquities in the British Museum." The quotes used in this chapter can be found in his translations, such as *The Book of the Dead* (1895), *The Chapters of Coming Forth by Day* (1898), and *The Egyptian Heaven and Hell* (1905). It's probably best to take Budge's translations with a grain of salt, though. He was a bit of a bluffer and had a habit of passing himself off as more fluent than he really was in various languages.

HIEROGLYPHICS

The ancient Egyptians wrote in hieroglyphics, but the word hieroglyphics is actually Greek—it means "sacred carvings." These sacred carvings started out as simple pictures—a dog meant "dog," an eye meant "eye." But over time, hieroglyphics became more complicated, with some characters taking on abstract meanings and others simply referring to sounds the same way our letters do.

After the Romans conquered Egypt, knowledge of hieroglyphics died out completely, and for a millennium and a half, no one could read the innumerable carvings on ancient Egypt's ruins.

In 1799, though, while most of French General Napoleon's soldiers in Egypt were getting captured or killed, one of them found an ancient tablet they called the Rosetta Stone. This stone had the same text written in Greek *and* in hieroglyphics. Since scholars could read Greek, they were able to puzzle out what some of the hieroglyphics meant, and this proved to be the key to piecing together three millennia's worth of Egyptian writing.

THE FIRST SHORT STORIES

The Ancient Egyptians are generally considered the first people to write fiction. Among the papyrus rolls dug up from the Egyptian sands are several short stories, similar to fairy tales. Many of them were collected by the French Egyptologist Gaston Maspero in *Popular Stories of Ancient Egypt* (1882), including the story "King Khufui and the Magicians."

One of the magicians who appears in the story, Didi of Didusanafrui, is "a hundred and ten years" old but every day eats a "hundred loaves with a whole leg of beef." Didi "knows how to make himself followed by a lion without a leash," but more impressively, "he knows how to put back in place a head that has been cut off."

To prove it, Didi once decapitated a goose and put the body on one side of a room and the head on the other. Then he recited some magic words, and "the goose rose up, it hopped, the head did the same, and when one had reunited with the other the goose began to cackle."

BEATRICE RAPPACCINI

FROM

"RAPPACCINI'S DAUGHTER"

BY NATHANIEL HAWTHORNE (1844)

Dr. Giacomo Rappaccini of the University of Padua was "a man fearfully acquainted with the secrets of nature." It was said that the good doctor cared "infinitely more for science than for mankind," but no one could deny his genius. His specialty was the cultivation and modification of poisonous plants, and his daughter Beatrice grew up in his garden of death.

Dr. Rappaccini created some of the exotic species by "mingling" parts of different plants, Frankenstein style. Although the pieces he used were "individually lovely," when they were combined, they showed a "questionable and ominous character." The most beautiful and deadly flower in the garden

CATEGORY: Science experiment

BASE OF OPERATIONS: Padua, Italy

WHEN: "Very long ago"

POWERS: The poison touch

WEAKNESS: Antivenom

MOST DASTARDLY DEED: So many dead insects!

FEAR FACTOR:

grew in its heart, a shrub sporting "a profusion of purple blossoms" with "the luster and richness of a gem."

This was Beatrice Rappaccini's twin sister.

Not literally, of course. Beatrice was not a plant! But the purple shrub and the baby girl were born the same day, and Beatrice was raised alongside the plant, "nourished with its breath." Beatrice loved the shrub "with a human affection." They were very much alike, these two. Both were achingly beautiful, and both were deadly.

This was Beatrice Rappaccini's curse: Her breath was poisonous; her touch was poisonous.

It wasn't all bad, of course. Mosquitoes never bothered her, because once they got close, they fell dead.

But it was mostly bad. Anyone foolish enough to touch Beatrice's skin came down with a "burning and tingling" rash. A kiss probably meant death; no one was sure because no one ever took the risk. Beatrice lived "estranged from all society."

She had her plants, of course—plants that only she could tend because their very odor would kill any other gardener. Her father was "said to have instructed her deeply in his science," and despite her youth, she was "already qualified to fill a professor's chair."

Perhaps Beatrice would have lived her whole life shut up in this "Eden of poisonous flowers." But one day, a student, Giovanni Guasconti, gained access to the garden. Giovanni was the first person (in fact, the first nonplant) her own age that Beatrice had ever met, so naturally they fell in love.

But it's hard to be in love when your touch is poisonous. Also poisonous: most of the plants in the place where you live. When Giovanni visited the garden, he had to be careful not to touch 1) his girlfriend, and 2) anything else.

Over time, hanging out in the garden began to have a strange effect on Giovanni. He'd walk down the street and flowers would wilt as he passed. Spiders died if he got too close. There was a "poison in his breath." He was becoming, as he put it, "a world's wonder of hideous monstrosity"—just like sweet Beatrice!

Giovanni had friends at the university, though, and he got one professor to whip up an antidote that would neutralize even "the most virulent poisons." Giovanni offered his beloved a drink, hoping to make her normal.

But Beatrice was poison all the way through. One sip of the antidote and there was nothing left of her. She keeled over dead.

BEYOND THE BOOK

THE ALL-TIME GREATEST LITERARY POISONINGS

Literature is full of clever poisonings, but the undisputed champion poisoners of literature all come from seventeenth-century English plays, such as:

- *The White Devil* by John Webster (1612). The Duke of Brachiano wants to bump off his loving wife. He knows that every night she kisses his portrait goodnight, so he has the portrait's lips coated with poison. One last goodnight kiss and no more wife.

- *The Revenger's Tragedy* by Thomas Middleton (1606). A wicked duke killed Vindice's wife with poison, so Vindice dresses the remnants of the poisoned corpse up like a living woman and tricks the duke into thinking it's his girlfriend. The duke kisses the skull—and dies from the poison.

- *Hamlet* by William Shakespeare (ca. 1600). Famously, Claudius kills the sleeping king of Denmark by pouring poison into his ear. Not as cunning as Brachiano's or Vindice's plans, but just as effective!

Three perfect crimes! But actually, no one gets away with anything in seventeenth-century drama, so Brachiano, Vindice, and Claudius all bite the dust eventually (two by poison: Brachiano puts on a poisoned helmet, and Claudius is stabbed with a poisoned sword. Vindice just gets his head cut off, no poison involved).

ON POISONS

"Mr. Henbane, the toxicologist . . . has passed half his life in studying poisons and antidotes. The first thing he did on his arrival here was to kill the cat; and while Miss Crotchet was crying over her, he brought her to life again."

—From *Crotchet Castle*
by Thomas Love Peacock (1831)

THE MOST POISONOUS BOOK OF ALL

In the nineteenth century, arsenic was often used as a component of green paints on wallpaper. Over time, the wallpaper would shed toxic arsenic dust. This was not healthy.

In an attempt to raise awareness of the dangers of deadly wallpaper, Dr. Robert Kedzie bound a bunch of wallpaper samples into a book and slapped a poison warning on it, calling it *Shadows from the Walls of Death*. He then sent one hundred free copies to various libraries around Michigan.

Most libraries discarded the dangerous book, but a few kept their copies in storage. Over the next century, as more and more arsenic flaked off of the oversize pages, the surviving volumes became deadlier and deadlier. Every page turned sent out a toxic billow of arsenic dust.

The wallpaper samples were beautiful, though. No nontoxic pigment creates such a lovely shade of green.

CHEOPS

FROM
THE MUMMY!
BY JANE WEBB (1827)

Long ago, in ancient Egypt, a "gigantic but well-proportioned" pharaoh named Cheops fell in love with his own sister and killed his own father and generally had a guilty conscience when he died. Priests wrapped him up in "innumerable folds of red and white linen" and deposited his mummy in a secret room in the Great Pyramid of Giza. There he lay undiscovered for 4,700 years.

In the year 2126, his secret tomb was located and opened, and two British scientists traveled by airship to Egypt with "the most compendious and powerful galvanic battery ever yet beheld by mortal." They hypothesized that "by employing so powerful an agent as galvanism, re-animation may be produced."

CATEGORY: Undead

BASE OF OPERATIONS:
Egypt, then England

WHEN: AD 2126

POWERS: Superstrength;
preternatural cunning

MOST DASTARDLY DEED:
Bending everyone to his will
(but also patricide)

FEAR FACTOR:

In other words, they planned to shock the mummy to life.

In the heart of the pyramid, Dr. Entwerfen and his young assistant Edric Montagu fastened a battery to the royal mummy. While a thunderstorm roared about the pyramids, "shaking their enormous masses to the foundation," the mummy opened ancient eyes "shining with supernatural luster."

Entwerfen ran away in blind panic, but Montagu stood paralyzed by its gaze. Suddenly, "dry, bony fingers" grabbed Montagu, and the mummy pulled himself upright. Standing tall for the first time in 4,700 years, Cheops staggered out of the pyramid and into the storm. "What place is this?" he shouted.

"Methinks all seems wondrous, new, and strange!"

And what did he see but the scientists' airship! Not knowing what it was, he stumbled aboard, and the airship's autopilot drew him up and away, on the long trip back to England.

Entwerfen and Montagu could only gape in astonishment as the mummy sailed away. They had unleashed a "fearful specter" upon the world, a fiend "in whose bosom dwells everlasting fire."

When Cheops disembarked in London, he found a futuristic wonderworld. Cooks, surgeons, and prison guards were all windup mechanical "automata." Letters were sent great distances quickly by a

relay system in hollowed-out cannonballs fired from great "steam-cannon."
Fashionable women wore "gossamer nets made of the spider's web," and hats
equipped with "very pretty fountains made of glass dust" that were "thrown
up in little jets by a small perpetual motion wheel."

The sudden arrival of a gigantic being with eyes "like fire" created chaos
in the court of the Queen of England, and an assassin took advantage of the
tumult to poison the queen. A new queen had to be chosen, and in the rush
of intrigue and backstabbing, Cheops found himself in his element.

For months he lurked in the shadows, "muffled in a thick cloak,"
clambering over walls and slipping through windows to advise and
manipulate the conspirators. He was a terrifying sight when he cast his cloak
off, for "his fearful eyes . . . seemed to possess the fabled fascination of those
of the rattle-snake" and his laugh was "like the yell of a demon."

As he was stronger, faster, and more cunning than any man living, the
mummy had every faction in the court of England dancing to his tune as he
manipulated them into betraying each other and themselves in turn.

And yet, at the end of all his tricks and machinations, the apparently sinister mummy left "the United Kingdoms of Great Britain and Ireland" stable and at peace. He explained to Edric Montagu that he had spent the millennia in "eternal misery" from guilt over the crimes of his life—the dead father, the romanced sister—and "a wild, never-dying fiend" raged in his heart, burning "with unquenchable fire and never-ceasing torment."

To ease his guilty conscience, Cheops had sought to bring the twenty-second century under a rule of just law.

"Permitted for a time to revisit earth," the mummy told Montagu, "I have made use of the powers entrusted to me to assist the good and punish the malevolent. Under pretense of aiding them, I gave them counsels which only plunged them yet deeper in destruction, whilst the evil that my advice appeared to bring upon the good was only like a passing cloud before the sun: it gave luster to the success that followed. My task is now finished." Then the mummy returned to the Great Pyramid, crawled into his coffin, and fell back into eternal slumber.

In the twenty-second century, at least, a monster can save the world and not seek to destroy it.

THE WORLD OF 2126

In the late twentieth century, science fiction started depicting retro-futuristic, Victorian worlds with advanced technology inspired by the nineteenth century. This subgenre eventually became known as *steampunk*. *The Mummy!*, with its use of the "steam-cannon," the "steam digging-machine," and the "steam-percussion-moveable bridge," deserves a tip of the top hat for being steampunk *avant la lettre*—"before the word existed."

BEYOND THE BOOK

OTHER LITERARY MUMMIES

After the Rosetta stone (see p. 7) helped linguists decipher hieroglyphics in the early nineteenth century, knowledge of the long-vanished culture exploded. A fad for ancient Egyptian art and culture swept Europe, and many writers incorporated mummies into their books.

- **"Lot No. 249"** by Arthur Conan Doyle (1892). An Oxford undergraduate figures out a way to animate an Egyptian mummy and send it on missions of vengeance against school rivals. Among the strangest things about "Lot No. 249" is the revelation that, in the late nineteenth century, Oxford students were allowed to keep mummies in their dorm rooms, provided they were for educational purposes.

- **"The Mummy's Foot"** by Théophile Gautier (1840). One day a man purchases a mummy's foot to use as a paperweight, but when he takes it home it begins to hop around as though "it had suddenly been brought into contact with a galvanic battery." The foot leaps back to the mummy it came from, which has limped into the room. You'll notice that a galvanic battery is, in fact, exactly what is "brought into contact with" Cheops in *The Mummy!*

- **"Some Words with a Mummy"** by Edgar Allan Poe (1845). This satire features a whiny, unimpressed mummy who is revived with "a battery." "The application of electricity to a mummy three or four thousand years old at the least, was an idea, if not very sage, still sufficiently original," explains the narrator, which is dead wrong—Jane Webb thought of shocking a mummy into life in 1827, so "original" is one thing this idea is not.

DEVILFISH

FROM

TWENTY THOUSAND LEAGUES UNDER THE SEA

BY JULES VERNE (1870)

Four hundred fifty million years ago, cephalopods ruled the seas. It's been downhill for them ever since. There are still plenty of cephalopods, of course—octopuses and squid, most notably—but those pesky fish, with their bones and their red blood cells, have long since taken over the oceans. The surviving cephalopods are those that are good at hiding, or that live in places that fish rarely dare to go.

In the bone-crushing ocean deeps, for example, where the sunlight cannot reach, fish are nothing but terrified, scuttling prey before the one mollusk that still reigns supreme: the giant squid.

Mariners used to call such squid "devilfish," and were terrified of the beasts, even though they rarely come to the ocean's

CATEGORY: Animal

BASE OF OPERATIONS:
The abysmal sea

WHEN: The last several million years

POWERS: Look at all those arms!

MOST DASTARDLY DEED:
Eating a French guy

FEAR FACTOR: 💀💀💀💀

surface. They lurk deep down, completely out of reach . . . unless you have some kind of submarine.

Enter Captain Nemo, the genius inventor of a deadly submarine called the *Nautilus*. He was also an international criminal, terrorist, and freedom fighter dedicated to ending British imperialism. The son of an Indian raja from Bundelkhand, Nemo trolled the seas in his *Nautilus*, ramming "imperialistic" ships from underwater with his submarine's pointed prow.

When the *Nautilus* ventured into deep waters, Captain Nemo had the honor of facing off against a "stupendous kraken"—not just one, but a herd, each with tentacles more than fifty feet long, that wrapped their giant arms around the submarine.

Bullets from the ship's guns just bounced off of their rubbery bodies, so the ship surfaced, innumerable tentacles still clinging to its sides, and Nemo opened a hatch. He knew the ways of devilfish, and he decided "to fight them at close quarters."

Armed with axes and one harpoon, the crew of the *Nautilus* faced off against "ten or twelve" beasts, each with eight tentacles. (Giant squid actually have ten tentacles, so Nemo must have miscounted.) Each tentacle struck "like a snake" and had 250 suckers that could stick to the victim like vacuums. "With flailing axes," Nemo and his crew started severing tentacles, which landed, writhing, on the deck. The harpooner threw his spear to "plunge into a squid's sea-green eye and burst it."

But in the middle of this carnage, one sailor was encircled by a tentacle and "glued to its suckers." "Brandishing its victim like a feather," the devilfish waved him in the air as Nemo and his crew amputated its colossal limbs. They managed to hack off seven tentacles before the devilfish vomited up a cloud of ink and, while everyone was blinded, slipped away into the ocean, its prisoner in tow.

Soon the other devilfish followed it in flight. The squid were exceptionally quick in everything they did, "thanks to their owning a triple heart."

We are assured that "the arms and tails of these animals grow back through regeneration," so don't worry about the devilfish. The devilfish turned out all right.

The *Nautilus*, though, was short one crewman.

SEA VAMPIRE

Author Victor Hugo imagined that the devilfish is a "sea vampire." In his book *Toilers of the Sea* (1866), he claims that the devilfish is "partly fish, partly reptile" and that the suckers on its tentacles are little mouths used to suck the blood of its victims. "A glutinous mass, endowed with a malignant will, what can be more horrible?"

None of this is a very accurate description of any real cephalopod, but Hugo wanted his hero to fight one, so he made it scary.

BEYOND THE BOOK

IN THE BELLY OF THE BEAST

Who gets swallowed by a sea monster? Jonah in the Bible did it first ("and Jonah was in the belly of the fish three days and three nights"), but he wasn't the last. Other victims appear in:

- **Cinque Canti** by Ludovico Ariosto (1545). In this epic poem, a sequel to the more famous *Orlando Furioso*, the brave knights Ruggierio and Astolfo get swallowed by a sorceress's pet whale. Ariosto never finished the poem, so we don't know if they ever get out.

- **The Adventures of Pinocchio** by Carlo Collodi (1883). Both the puppet Pinocchio and his father are swallowed (on separate occasions) by the enormous Dog-fish. Fortunately, the Dog-fish is asthmatic, and sleeps with its mouth open, so they are able to clamber out and swim to safety. (It's different in the movie.)

- **Just So Stories** by Rudyard Kipling (1902). When a whale swallows a shipwrecked sailor, raft and all, the sailor kicks and stomps around in its stomach so much that the nauseous whale agrees to let him go. On his way out, the sailor fashions a grate out of the remnants of his raft and sticks it in the whale's throat. "And that is the reason why whales nowadays never eat men or boys or little girls." So there will be no more of that!

ON THE ORIGIN OF SUPERVILLAINS

Jules Verne was a guy with a lot of ideas. Scientists getting shot to the moon from a giant cannon! An electric submarine! A journey through caves to the center of the Earth!

One of Jules Verne's ideas is still wildly popular today: supervillains. Captain Nemo is a brilliant scientist who uses his inventions to terrorize the world.

In *Robur the Conqueror* (1886) and *Master of the World* (1904), the Master terrorizes lesser scientists with flying inventions his henchmen build in their secret island hideout. Even in the early short story "A Voyage in a Balloon" (1851), Verne writes of a mad scientist who brags about his knowledge ("I have searched all, comprehended all!") and plans, in a fit of madness, both to fly a balloon into the sun and also to "crush" the people who have rejected his genius. That's pure supervillainy right there!

There would be no Lex Luthor or Doctor Doom without Jules Verne. He invented the supervillain.

THE KRAKEN

Alfred, Lord Tennyson's famous poem "The Kraken" (1830) depicts a gigantic sea squid that has slept underwater since the dawn of time. Only on the world's last day will he rise from the deeps.

> *Below the thunders of the upper deep,*
> *Far, far beneath in the abysmal sea,*
> *His ancient, dreamless, uninvaded sleep*
> *The Kraken sleepeth: faintest sunlights flee*
> *About his shadowy sides; above him swell*
> *Huge sponges of millennial growth and height;*
> *And far away into the sickly light,*
> *From many a wondrous grot and secret cell*
> *Unnumbered and enormous polypi*
> *Winnow with giant arms the slumbering green.*
> *There hath he lain for ages, and will lie*
> *Battening upon huge sea worms in his sleep,*
> *Until the latter fire shall heat the deep;*
> *Then once by man and angels to be seen,*
> *In roaring he shall rise and on the surface die.*

Notice how Tennyson draws attention to the final line by making it longer; it has two more syllables than all of the other lines, or to put it technically, the last line is written in iambic hexameter (twelve syllables per line), while the other lines are written in iambic pentameter (ten syllables). Keats uses the same trick in the lines quoted from "The Lamia" on page 115. A hexameter line like this is called an "alexandrine."

DORIAN GRAY

FROM

THE PICTURE OF DORIAN GRAY

BY OSCAR WILDE (1890)

Pity poor Dorian Gray! He was young, handsome, wealthy, and beloved by all, but he was cursed with a terrible fate: Someday he would grow old.

That doesn't sound so bad, really. After all, everyone grows old. But Dorian was really quite handsome and lovable.

When his friend, the painter Basil Hallward, produced his "masterpiece"—a life-size picture of Dorian Gray—Dorian found himself "jealous of the portrait," just as he was "jealous of everything whose beauty does not die." How unjust that Dorian Gray the man would grow old, that someday "his face would be wrinkled and wizen, his eyes dim and colorless, the

CATEGORY: Cursed human

BASE OF OPERATIONS: London

WHEN: The late nineteenth century

POWERS: Immortality; being ridiculously handsome

WEAKNESS: Vanity

MOST DASTARDLY DEEDS: Murder and blackmail

FEAR FACTOR: 💀💀💀

grace of his figure broken and deformed," while the painting would remain forever youthful.

"If it were only the other way!"

And just like that, Dorian got his wish. From that moment on, Dorian ceased to age. He took the painting home with him, hung it on his wall, and never grew a day older.

Soon after, Dorian met Lord Henry Wotton, a man of taste and a cynic. Lord Henry told Dorian that "beauty is a form of genius—is higher, indeed, than genius"; that "youth is the one thing worth having"; that "no civilized man ever regrets a pleasure, and no uncivilized man ever knows what a pleasure is." Lord Henry had lots of advice, and it was all bad.

Under Lord Henry's influence, Dorian started behaving badly. He broke the heart of his girlfriend Sibyl Vane, and in grief, she took her own life.

And when Dorian glanced at Basil's painting on his wall, look! Upon the portrait, the face of Dorian Gray now had a wicked grin of "vicious cruelty."

Dorian realized that he could do whatever he wanted without consequence, leaving the painting "to bear the burden of his shame." And it was all downhill from there.

"Eternal youth, infinite passion, pleasures subtle and secret, wild joys and wilder sins"—that was Dorian's life.

For eighteen years, Dorian indulged in every wickedness under the sun, and none of it touched him. It only touched the "evil and aging face on the canvas." The portrait became so twisted-looking that Dorian hid it in an attic room.

But word got around about Dorian Gray. Decent people would not be seen with him. Decent restaurants would not serve him.

One day, Basil Hallward visited his old friend. He had heard disturbing rumors—eighteen years' worth of disturbing rumors!—and he wanted to know if they were true. Dorian Gray had such a "pure, bright, innocent face" that the "most dreadful things" they'd been saying about him couldn't possibly be accurate!

With a "bitter laugh," Dorian took Basil upstairs and showed him the portrait, after which he killed him.

Finally, after many more years of corruption and blackmail, after many more ruined lives and dead bodies on his conscience, Dorian Gray decided he'd had enough of vice. He resolved to reform.

LORD HENRY'S BEST QUIPS

"Nowadays most people die of a sort of creeping common sense, and discover when it is too late that the only things one never regrets are one's mistakes."

"The reason we all like to think so well of others is that we are all afraid for ourselves. The basis of optimism is sheer terror."

"It is only shallow people who do not judge by appearances. The true mystery of the world is the visible, not the invisible."

But the painting, for all its subject's good intentions, still showed an aging, dissolute, evil murderer. Dorian could vow repentance all he wanted: The truth was in that portrait! So, to rid the world of this one shred of evidence of his evil, Dorian stabbed the painting with a knife.

A scream rang out.

When servants and police broke into the attic room, they found "hanging upon the wall a splendid portrait" of a young and beautiful Dorian Gray. Next to it, lying on the floor, was a "withered, wrinkled, and loathsome" corpse "with a knife in his heart."

So passed the immortal Dorian Gray.

BEYOND THE BOOK

THE SINS OF DORIAN GRAY

Dorian Gray is always indulging in "vice" or "crime," but what exactly is he doing? The book spends more words describing Dorian in the act of researching perfumes or medieval tapestries than it does describing him in the act of doing something "evil."

Oscar Wilde was in a pickle. He wanted to write about a "wicked" character, but Victorian novelists were supposed to produce work that was rated G, or at worst PG. Like Mr. Hyde (see page 90), Dorian Gray runs all around London getting into trouble—but exactly what kind of trouble can never be spoken.

When Dorian Gray starts killing people, things snap into place. But before that, readers must use their imaginations. And those imaginations got Oscar Wilde in trouble! Contemporary reviewers called this book immoral. Oscar Wilde replied, "There is no such thing as a moral or an immoral book. Books are well written, or badly written. That is all."

OSCAR WILDE AND THE READING GAOL GAMBIT

Years after writing *The Picture of Dorian Gray*, Oscar Wilde found himself tarred by scandal and shunned for the time he'd spent in prison. He lived in poverty, as no one would publish his writing.

Finally, he produced a long anonymous poem, "The Ballad of Reading Gaol" (1898), about the cruel conditions he had experienced in prison (gaol is the British spelling for jail). Freed from the scandalous name of Wilde, the poem became a surprise hit.

> *I know not whether Laws be right,*
> *Or whether Laws be wrong;*
> *All that we know who lie in gaol*
> *Is that the wall is strong;*
> *And that each day is like a year,*
> *A year whose days are long.*

DRACULA

FROM

DRACULA

BY BRAM STOKER (1897)

In a decaying castle in Transylvania lurked a man with "the strength in his hand of twenty men." His will commanded "the storm, the fog, the thunder," as well as "the rat, and the owl, and the bat—the moth, and the fox, and the wolf." He could change shape and size and assume the form of a bat or a wolf or a mist. He moved "panther-like" and with "diabolical quickness." He could clamber up vertical surfaces "just as a lizard moves along a wall." And—most terrifying of all—he was "without heart or conscience," and knew "no fear and no remorse."

No, wait. Actually, what was most terrifying of all was the fact that he was a vampire.

His name, of course, was Dracula. And Dracula had a plan.

CATEGORY: Undead

BASE OF OPERATIONS: Today Transylvania, tomorrow the world!

WHEN: The span of several centuries

POWERS: Yikes! So many!

WEAKNESS: Cannot survive decapitation, or being stabbed in the heart. But who can?

MOST DASTARDLY DEED: RIP, Lucy

FEAR FACTOR: 💀 💀💀 💀 💀

"MY REVENGE IS JUST BEGUN! I SPREAD IT OVER CENTURIES, AND TIME IS ON MY SIDE."

—COUNT DRACULA

First he hired an English lawyer, Jonathan Harker, to come to Transylvania and arrange for the purchase of several properties in London. Then he hopped a ship and sailed to his new home, leaving Harker behind to be eaten by three female vampires who lived in his castle.

In England, Dracula went into action. He started feeding on a lovely young woman named Lucy Westenra, who was newly engaged. Night by night, Lucy grew weaker as our hero, Count Dracula, drained her blood.

Unfortunately for our hero's plans, Jonathan Harker had not been eaten, but rather escaped Castle Dracula and spent months crawling back to England. And his wife just happened to be Lucy Westenra's best friend.

Even more unfortunately, Lucy's ex-boyfriend knew the Dutch doctor Abraham Van Helsing, "a philosopher and a metaphysician, and one of the most advanced scientists of his day." Van Helsing knew what English scientists did not—to wit, something about vampires.

Lucy's mysterious illness, an anemia that worsened every night, brought Abraham Van Helsing, "M.D., D.Ph., D.Lit., etc., etc.," sailing across the English Channel to diagnose the patient. Between Harker and Van Helsing, it didn't take long for everyone to figure out what was happening to Lucy. A vampire was happening.

Too late for Lucy, though. She died of blood loss, came back as a vampire, and started feeding on the local children.

So Van Helsing and a ragtag band of Lucy's ex-boyfriends dug up her coffin and found her corpse there, looking blooming and fresh, but with the addition of "the pointed teeth, the bloodstained, voluptuous mouth." Van Helsing knew what to do with a vampire. You must "cut off his head and burn his heart or drive a stake through it." So that's what they did to Lucy. One down, one to go.

Count Dracula was not so easy to locate, however. And he had already moved on to his next victim: Harker's wife, Mina.

Jonathan Harker desperately sought the vampire throughout London. Every time Harker or Van Helsing uncovered one of Dracula's hiding places, they would bless the area with holy items, which the unholy Count could not bear. But he was always one step ahead of them, and they never found his sleeping form.

"That wonderful Madam Mina," meanwhile, had an idea. Thanks to the feastings, she and Dracula shared a psychic bond. If Dr. Van Helsing were to hypnotize her, perhaps he could tunnel through that psychic bond and unearth clues about Dracula's whereabouts.

Fortunately, Van Helsing was a "student of the brain" and therefore a master hypnotist. He stood before Mina and began "to make passes in front of her, from over the top of her head downward, with each hand in turn." Soon she was in a trance and perceived . . .

A ship. Our hero was in a coffin on a ship. He was going home.

Everyone raced to Transylvania. They planned to take advantage of the fact that Dracula was powerless in the daylight—the sun didn't kill him, as rumor would have it, but it did make him no stronger than a normal human. If they could catch up to his coffin as it was transported through Romania to Castle Dracula, killing the old man would be simple—if it was daytime.

VAMPIRES IN A NUTSHELL

"The amphibious existence of the vampire is sustained by daily renewed slumber in the grave. Its horrible lust for living blood supplies the vigor of its waking existence. It will never desist until it has satiated its passion, and drained the very life of its coveted victim."

—From Carmilla by Joseph Sheridan Le Fanu (1872)

It was not so easy to catch up to Dracula, though. The Count had planned his route so well that by the time the vampire hunters reached their prey, it was almost dusk, and the coffin was outside the walls of Castle Dracula.

The Count's henchmen were "flogging the horses" at full gallop. Snow began "falling more heavily." Wolves came rushing down from the mountains "in twos and threes and larger numbers." Each henchman drew a "knife or pistol" and prepared to fight.

The vampire hunters came with Winchester rifles, though, and were able to hold off Dracula's minions long enough to knock the coffin from the back of the wagon. They drew their knives, and while Jonathan Harker lopped the Count's head off, Quincey Morris (one of the ex-boyfriends) drove his knife into Dracula's heart. Morris got stabbed to death by one of the henchmen in the process. But too late! Count Dracula's body crumbled "into dust."

BEYOND THE BOOK

DEAR DRACULA

Up through the early nineteenth century, many novels were "epistolary novels" that took the form of a series of letters. The entire text of *Frankenstein* (1818), for example, is a letter written by an arctic explorer to his sister, to which he has attached Victor Frankenstein's confessions.

Dracula is innovative in that it contains diary entries, letters, ship logs, newspaper clippings, telegrams, and transcriptions of "phonograph" records all gathered together like a dossier of evidence. It looks at first more like someone's research files than a novel—possibly Dr. Van Helsing's?

By building a book around documents, Bram Stoker lends verisimilitude to an otherwise completely unbelievable story. That is, he makes the story appear to be true, even though we know it's just a novel.

THE GRISLY TALE OF ELIZABETH SIDDAL

Dante Gabriel Rossetti, one of the most celebrated artists of the late nineteenth century, is also a famous poet—but he almost wasn't. While his paintings brought him fame, he only showed his poems to his friends. He occasionally sent love poems to women he knew, too, and when his wife, Elizabeth Siddal, learned about those, she died of heartbreak.

Rossetti, in repentance, vowed never to write poetry again. He placed every poem he had ever written on his wife's corpse, above her heart, and crossed her hands over them. Then he buried her. Seven years passed.

One day, one of Rossetti's friends asked him what had ever become of those poems he used to show around. They were really good. Rossetti had the makings (he said) of a great poet.

That was enough for Rossetti! He had his wife dug up. Her skeletal fingers had grown stiff over the pages, and Rossetti had to break them to reclaim his poems. He published them and became famous.

Around that time, a rumor went around Britain (probably false) that Elizabeth Siddal Rossetti had been perfectly preserved when she was dug up. Bram Stoker was a neighbor of Rossetti's and knew all about the exhumation (digging up). The story of the preserved corpse was one of his inspirations for *Dracula*. The beautiful Elizabeth Siddal was the model for the character Lucy.

BEFORE DRACULA

Vampires were incredibly popular throughout the nineteenth century, and *Dracula* is just the capstone of a century of blood-drinking stories. Such as:

- **Christabel** by Samuel Taylor Coleridge (1816). Young Christabel lives with her father in an isolated castle. One day, they take in Geraldine, a mysterious woman "most beautiful to see." But there's something weird about Geraldine. The dog hates her. She can "the bodiless dead espy" (she can see ghosts). And she has a strange, malignant power over Christabel. Although Coleridge never says that Geraldine is a vampire, she sure acts like a vampire. She certainly influenced all the vampire stories that came after.

- **"The Vampyre"** by John Polidori (1819). The same dare that produced *Frankenstein* (see p. 55) also produced this vampire tale. The vampire, Lord Ruthven, is a gentleman who feasts on the blood of beautiful women, and the story is similar to a poorly written version of *Dracula*, with one wonderful difference: Lord Ruthven always wins! No one can stop him, and he just feasts on any character he wants and then slips away.

- **Carmilla** by Joseph Sheridan Le Fanu (1872). In rural Austria, a nobleman lives in a castle with his young daughter, Laura. One day, there is a carriage accident on the road nearby, and the family takes in a recovering girl just about Laura's age. This is Carmilla, and she and Laura become inseparable—at least in part because Carmilla is secretly a vampire, and every night she sneakily drinks Laura's blood. (You can tell Le Fanu borrowed a lot from *Christabel*!)

FAFNIR

FROM

THE VOLSUNG SAGA

(13TH CENTURY)

In "the waste of Gnita-heath," on the world's largest treasure hoard, there brooded the dragon Fafnir.

Fafnir hadn't always been a dragon. Once he had been the eldest of the three sons of Hreidmar. Among his brothers, Fafnir was "by far the greatest and grimmest, and would have all things about called his."

And then one day, wandering gods accidentally killed Fafnir's younger brother Otter.

Now, in those days, if you killed someone, you had to pay a *weregild* to the dead person's family—a tax to make up for the crime. The gods swiped the gold they needed from a nearby dwarf, even taking the ring from his finger.

CATEGORY: Cursed human

BASE OF OPERATIONS: Gnita-heath

WHEN: The 6th century, maybe

POWERS: Poison breath, deadly blood

MOST DASTARDLY DEEDS: Patricide; hoarding

FEAR FACTOR: 💀💀💀💀

The dwarf cursed the gods: "That gold-ring, yea and all the gold withal, should be the bane of every man who should own it thereafter."

The gods gave the ring and all the gold to Hreidmar, and he was satisfied. He was now a rich man—but not for long. His eldest son Fafnir killed him and took the gold away to Gnita-heath. There Fafnir sat on the treasure and "so became the worst of all worms"—that is to say, he turned into a dragon.

Fafnir spent his days guarding his hoard. When people approached, he would "spout out poison, so that none durst come anigh [dared come near]," or he would scare them away with his "countenance of terror." No matter how many men came against him, he was always stronger than all of them. He had nothing to fear. He lived with his treasure and his ring, and let us suppose he was happy.

Meanwhile, the youngest Hreidmarsson brother, Regin, was not very happy. He had lost his father and one brother, and now his other brother had absconded with the gold without giving him a share. Regin was in no condition to fight a dragon himself, so he enlisted a young man named Sigurd Sigmundsson, who was unmatched in "growth and goodliness." Regin

forged Sigurd a sword that could cleave an anvil "down to the stock." This was a sword that could kill a dragon, even a dragon as mighty as Fafnir.

Sigurd and Regin rode to Gnita-heath, and for the first time, Sigurd saw the tracks Fafnir made, and became aware of the monster's great size. How would he kill such a beast?

Regin had a plan. He told Sigurd to dig a pit between Fafnir's cave and his watering hole. If Sigurd hopped into the pit, then when Fafnir slithered overhead, Sigurd could stab him in the belly. Regin hoped that the dragon's hot blood would pour out and boil Sigurd alive, thereby eliminating the only other person who knew about the treasure.

But Sigurd instead dug three deep channels, so when he stood in one and stabbed the dragon, the blood flowed down into the other two and left Sigurd untouched. Soon Fafnir's blood was gushing down the channels, while Sigurd calmly wiped the gore from his sword.

Regin then tried to kill Sigurd to claim all the gold for himself, but that didn't go well. Soon Sigurd was wiping his sword clean again.

And so Sigurd ended up with the gold, and the ring . . . and the curse.

BEYOND THE BOOK

DRAGON VS. ELEPHANT

The medieval scholar Bartholomeus Anglicus writes in his encyclopedic *On the Properties of Things* (1240), "Between elephants and dragons is everlasting fighting, for the dragon with his tail bindeth and spanneth the elephant, and the elephant with his foot and with his nose throweth down the dragon." The overheated dragon attacks so it can quench its thirst on the elephant's blood—for elephants have notoriously cool blood, and "the dragon is a full thirsty beast."

Joshua Sylvester, in his 1592 poem "Birth of the World," specifies that the dragon preys on elephants by thrusting "his nose, then head and all" into the elephant's trunk. Unable to breathe, the elephant suffocates to death.

Medieval bestiaries ("books of beasts") suggest that when a dragon wants to kill an elephant, it simply winds its tail around the poor beast and crushes it like a boa constrictor. Since bestiaries often used animals as metaphors and moral lessons, the bestiary goes on to state that the dragon represents sin, which acts as a snare and tangles people up, crushing them with guilt.

IN THE DARKNESS BIND THEM

A cursed ring . . . a dragon's hoard. . . . J. R. R. Tolkien was a medieval scholar who translated *Beowulf* and knew the Norse sagas well. So if it looks as though some aspects of these stories made their way into *The Hobbit* or *The Lord of the Rings*, don't be surprised. In fact, the name *Gandalf* comes directly from Old Norse literature (where it's the name of a dwarf).

THE DRAGONS OF GREEK MYTHOLOGY

Dragons appear in the legends of places all over the world, from Ethiopia to China. Ancient Greece was crawling with them!

- **Python** from "The Hymn to Apollo" by Cynaethus of Chios (ca. 522 BC). This "bloated, great she-dragon" was the daughter of the goddess Hera, born to Hera alone, with no father, simply because Hera was angry with her husband, Zeus. The baby Apollo (Zeus's son) slew Python with his bow and arrows, and established an oracle—the famous Oracle of Delphi—on the spot to commemorate the deed. Pythons, the snakes you might find in Africa or Southeast Asia, are named after this dragon.

- **The Ismenian Dragon** from the *Library* by Apollodorus (ca. the second century). When Cadmus was building the city of Thebes, a dragon at a nearby spring ate his friends. Cadmus slew the dragon, but now there was no one to live in Cadmus's city—the dragon had eaten them all. So Cadmus plucked the teeth from the dragon and sowed them like seeds. Men sprung up from the furrows and began to fight. The survivors became the first citizens of Cadmus's city and the ancestors of the people of Thebes.

- **The Dragon of the Grove of Ares** from the *Argonautica* by Apollonius of Rhodes (ca. 250 BC). When Jason, of Argonaut fame, sought to seize the Golden Fleece from the Grove of Ares, he found it guarded by a dragon. Although "neither by day nor by night does sweet sleep subdue his restless eyes," the dragon was nevertheless knocked out by Medea's spells, and Jason swiped the Fleece.

FRANKENSTEIN'S MONSTER

FROM

FRANKENSTEIN

BY MARY SHELLEY (1818)

As the rain pelted down on his attic laboratory, a young scientist toiled late into the night, meticulously stitching together a man out of the corpses he stole from graveyards, slaughterhouses, and dissecting rooms—human corpses, but perhaps some animal corpses, too, for what else can be found in a slaughterhouse? This was Victor Frankenstein, a chemistry student in eighteenth-century Germany and the world's first mad scientist.

Turns out that building a human from jumbled parts is difficult, and knitting together veins and nerves requires a delicate touch. To make his work easier, Victor constructed everything on a larger-than-life scale: The body he ended up building was a full eight feet tall

CATEGORY: Organic construct; science experiment

BASE OF OPERATIONS: All over Europe

WHEN: 18th century

POWERS: Resistance to cold

MOST DASTARDLY DEED: Killing everyone his father loved

FEAR FACTOR: 👾👾👾👾

In order to prevent anyone else from attempting to replicate his experiment, Victor refused to disclose how he managed to imbue dead flesh with the "spark of existence"—but somehow he did it! His creation lived!

Victor thought he would make a beautiful, giant man, but the creature turned out as hideous as any jigsaw puzzle of dead flesh. The end result was not a man but a monster, with watery yellow eyes and sallow skin that "scarcely covered the work of muscles and arteries beneath." Horrified by what he made, Victor fled from the monster, and by the time he worked up the nerve to return to his lab, the creature was gone.

WHAT'S HIS NAME?

If you ever refer to the monster as "Frankenstein," some know-it-all will pop up and say, "Excuse me, but Frankenstein is the name of the scientist. You're talking about Frankenstein's monster." But is the know-it-all right? The book never calls the monster by a name. But Victor Frankenstein compares himself to the monster's "father," and if the monster is Frankenstein's son, what name would he have but Frankenstein? At the very least, almost all media released since the book's publication have called the monster "Frankenstein."

But where do you go if you're an eight-foot-tall freak of nature with no sense of the world? The monster started to wander Europe, but everywhere he went, people either ran away screaming or threw rocks at him until he left. He was alone in the world, and he experienced nothing but hatred and pain.

Finally, the poor wretch found shelter in a little abandoned hovel attached to a peasant cottage. Holing up there unseen, he spent the winter spying on people. By eavesdropping, he learned to speak French; by swiping books, he learned to read; and reading taught him all about the world.

Unfortunately, he was still really ugly. People assumed that ugly on the outside equaled ugly on the inside—that the monster's soul was "as hellish as his form, full of treachery and fiend-like malice." However, the monster behaved kindly for a while. He saved a little girl from drowning. He befriended an old blind man.

But then he ran into Victor Frankenstein's younger brother, and because 1) the little boy was repulsed by the monster's hideousness, and 2) he was related to Victor Frankenstein, the monster wrung his neck. Then he framed the maid, who was sentenced to death and hanged for the crime. Perhaps it was the cruelty of society, but Victor Frankenstein's creation ended up as twisted in his morality as he was in his anatomy.

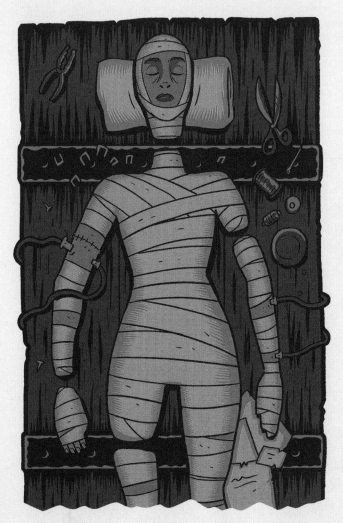

Lonely, depressed, "shunned and hated by all mankind," the monster came up with a plan. He tracked down Victor Frankenstein and demanded that his creator fashion another eight-foot-tall freak—to be his bride! The monster promised that he and his new wife would flee to the wilds of South America and live gentle, vegetarian lives.

This sounded like a good deal, so Victor agreed to kludge together a female monster. Eventually he chickened out, though, fearing that the two creatures might reproduce and spawn a "race of devils." Although he had half completed his assemblage of female body parts, he tore his work to pieces, dropping the chunks of flesh into the sea.

When he found out that he would not have his promised bride, the monster really went on a tear. He killed Victor's best friend. He waited until Victor got married and then killed Victor's wife on their wedding night. He didn't kill Victor's father, but all this death made the old man keel over dead from a broken heart anyway.

"I AM MALICIOUS BECAUSE I AM MISERABLE."
—FRANKENSTEIN'S MONSTER

Victor decided to devote his life to hunting down the murderous fiend he had made.

The monster led his creator on a merry chase, down to the Mediterranean and then up through Russia, farther and farther north, toward the "everlasting ices" of the North Pole.

Cold didn't bother the monster, but the farther north they went, the more Victor suffered. When temperature and exhaustion finally killed

off Victor Frankenstein, his monster came to his corpse and wept by the scientist's side.

The monster hated Victor, but his entire life had revolved around tormenting his creator. With Victor dead, what was left for the monster to do?

Nothing, that's what. So he vowed to set himself on fire, deep in the arctic wastes.

BEYOND THE BOOK

WHAT'S ON THE MONSTER'S SHELF?

Frankenstein's monster learned to read by puzzling through the books he found. These are the books he read:

- *The Sorrows of Young Werther* by Johann Wolfgang von Goethe (1774). The blockbuster bestseller of the eighteenth century, *Werther* tells the tragic tale of a sensitive young man whose doomed love drags him toward a tragic conclusion (spoiler: death). It was a book closely tied to a tragedy of Mary Shelley's family—it was the last book her mother read before she died.

- *Paradise Lost* by John Milton (1667). This epic poem details the story of Adam and Eve and the rebellion of Satan. It makes quite an impression on the monster, who sees himself as similar to Adam, "united by no link to any other being in existence." It must have made quite an impression on Mary Shelley as well, as she used three lines from it as the epigraph to her novel:

> Did I request thee, Maker, from my clay
> To mould me man? Did I solicit thee
> From darkness to promote me?

- **Plutarch's Lives** (ca. AD 100). The ancient historian Plutarch wrote this famous collection of parallel Greek and Roman biographies. He compares the life of Alexander the Great (Greek) to the life of Julius Caesar (Roman), for example, and the life of Theseus (the ancient Greek king who slew the Minotaur—see p. 169) to Romulus (the founder of Rome, who infamously slew his brother).

WHAT DOES THE MONSTER LOOK LIKE?

When you think of Frankenstein's monster, you probably think of neck-bolts, a flat-top, and clunky boots. This was the look that actor Boris Karloff sported in the 1931 movie adaptation, and it's become an iconic look. But that lurching creature bears little resemblance to the monster from the book—a gun-toting bookworm capable of moving "with the swiftness of lightning." This is how Shelley describes the monster:

> "No mortal could support the horror of that countenance. A mummy again endued with animation could not be so hideous as that wretch. I had gazed on him while unfinished; he was ugly then, but when those muscles and joints were rendered capable of motion, it became a thing such as even Dante could not have conceived."

> "I saw by the light of the moon the daemon at the casement. A ghastly grin wrinkled his lips . . . As I looked on him, his countenance expressed the utmost extent of malice and treachery."

WRITTEN ON A DARE

Mary Shelley is one of the youngest writers ever to produce a genuine classic. She was only eighteen when she wrote *Frankenstein*.

The story came to her while she was on vacation in Switzerland with her future husband, Percy Shelley, and their friends Lord Byron and Dr. John Polidori. The group was trapped in a Swiss château by bad weather, bored out of their skulls. Byron suggested that they each write a scary story to read to the group.

When Mary chose to write about someone who tried to create life and instead created a murderous monster who eventually did him in, she may have been thinking about her own mother, the great feminist writer Mary Wollstonecraft, who was indeed killed by her own creation: She died giving birth to Mary Shelley.

Four years after *Frankenstein* was published, Percy Shelley drowned in a boating accident, and the poet Leigh Hunt stole the heart from his corpse. Mary Shelley had to beg Hunt for the organ's return, almost the same way Victor Frankenstein had once scavenged for body parts.

THE GOBLIN SPIDER

FROM

JAPANESE FAIRY TALES

BY LAFCADIO HEARN (1899)

In Japan, "very ancient books" speak of haunted regions overrun by strange monsters and goblins known as *yokai*. There were many kinds of yokai in those days, such as the *kappa*, a turtle-man with a concave skull filled with water, and the *kasa-obake*, a hopping one-eyed umbrella. The most dreaded of the yokai, though, was the goblin spider, or *jorōgumo*.

When a regular spider lived for four hundred years, it got promoted to goblin spider. Goblin spiders looked "just like common spiders" during the day, but at night they grew to monstrous proportions and did "awful things." They had "the magical power of taking human shape—so as to deceive people."

CATEGORY: Shape-shifter

BASE OF OPERATIONS: Japan

WHEN: "Very ancient" times

POWERS: Webs

MOST DASTARDLY DEED:
Eating humans like flies

FEAR FACTOR: 💀💀💀

This was long ago, when every ruined building or forgotten grotto housed a yokai. And "in some lonely part of the country" there stood a "haunted temple."

The temple was abandoned, and for good reason. People who entered "were never heard of again." But people kept trying, as they do.

One day, a samurai "famous for his courage and his prudence" came looking for trouble. He entered the temple and hid under the altar.

Strange creatures passed by. A hideous goblin called out, "Hitokusai!" (see p. 141). But the samurai stayed hidden until he heard the beautiful music of a *samisen* (a Japanese instrument that looks like a banjo).

The samurai emerged from his hiding place and saw a priest playing the samisen. The music had an unearthly beauty, a haunting sound like no samisen the samurai had ever heard before.

The priest welcomed the samurai and explained that he played music at night "to keep off the goblins." He played for a while longer and then offered to let the samurai take a turn. The samurai was a suspicious man, but it seemed rude to decline. With his left hand, he reached for the samisen anyway . . .

. . . and as soon as he touched it, it turned into a handful of webs. The priest cast off his human disguise and stood revealed as a goblin spider!

KASA-OBAKE

The samurai tried to flee, but his left hand was stuck in the "monstrous spider web." So with his right hand, he drew his sword and hacked at the goblin spider as it closed in on him.

The wounded spider crawled away, but the samurai could not follow, for the more he struggled, the more he became entangled in the webs.

In the morning, the samurai's friends came looking for him and found him hanging in a snarl of cobwebs, weak but alive. They cut him loose and followed a trail of blood on the temple floor that led to a "deserted garden" nearby. From a hole in the garden came the moans of the spider. It, too, was weak but alive.

They took their rakes and shovels and finished it off, of course. There was no mercy for goblin spiders in those ancient days.

BEYOND THE BOOK

HYAKUMONOGATARI KAIDANKAI

In the story collection *Tonoigusa* by Ogita Ansei (1660), several samurai are playing the old Japanese game of Hyakumonogatari Kaidankai.

Here's how to play: Gather some friends and light one hundred candles in a dark room at night. Take turns telling ghost stories. At the end of your story, blow out a candle. As the night goes on, the number of candles dwindles, and the room gets darker and darker. After the hundredth terrifying story, the room is pitch black—if you're brave enough to make it that far.

In *Tonoigusa*, most of the samurai are (of course) terrified by the time the ninety-ninth candle is blown out. After the hundredth tale, as the teller reaches to snuff out the candle, a gigantic shadowy hand is seen on the wall. Panic in the room!

But one samurai draws his sword and cuts . . . a slender silken thread. The hand was actually the shadow cast by the legs of a spider as it lowered itself from the ceiling above the final candle. With its web cut, it fell into the flame. That's one less spider that will make it to four hundred.

HEARN

Lafcadio Hearn was an American newspaper reporter who took an assignment in Japan and decided to stay there, becoming a naturalized citizen. While teaching English and working for Japanese newspapers, he wrote many books and articles about Japan at a time (the nineteenth century) when Japan was little known in the English-speaking world. Among his most popular works are several books of traditional Japanese folktales, which he collected and translated.

Hearn also translated many French stories into English, including Gautier's "The Mummy's Foot" (see p. 19) and most of the works of Guy de Maupassant—although not, sadly, "The Horla" (see p. 78).

SPIDERS AT NIGHT

"A spider seen anywhere at night, the people say, should be killed; for all spiders that show themselves after dark are goblins. While people are awake and watchful, such creatures make themselves small; but when everybody is fast asleep, then they assume their true goblin shape and become monstrous."

—From "In a Japanese Garden" by Lafcadio Hearn (1892).

OTHER JAPANESE MONSTERS

A folktale Hearn recorded from a Japanese peasant (published in his collection *Kwaidan* in 1904) speaks of the Yuki-Onna, a "snow woman" who breathes on the faces of sleeping men in cold weather, her breath "like a bright white smoke." This freezes them solid and incidentally kills them.

Rokuro-Kubi (also from *Kwaidan*) are human-looking monsters whose heads come off at night and fly around "eating worms and insects" and any unsuspecting people they find. But if someone finds the body of the Rokuro-Kubi and moves it, "the head will never be able to join itself again to the neck." In fact, "when the head comes back and finds that its body has been moved, it will strike itself upon the floor three times,—bounding like a ball,— and will pant as in great fear, and presently die."

Kwaidan also tells of a monster known as a Jikininki, or "man-eating goblin." By day the Jikininki appears as a priest, but at night he reveals his "true shape," which is "dim and awful" and "vague and vast," and he eats corpses "more quickly than a cat devours a rat."

THE
GOLEM

FROM
THE GOLEM
BY GUSTAV MEYRINK (1915)

Long ago, in the city of Prague, a learned rabbi made a man-shaped figure out of clay, and on its forehead, he wrote the Hebrew word *'emeth*, or "truth." Various magical incantations brought the clay figure to life.

The Golem could not speak, but it understood and followed directions, and the rabbi used it as a servant to tidy up around the synagogue and run errands. The Golem would start out small, but it grew taller and taller over the course of the week. Every Friday evening the rabbi rubbed out the beginning of the word on the creature's forehead with his thumb, leaving only *meth*—the Hebrew word for "death"—and the Golem collapsed into a clay heap. After the Sabbath, the rabbi would create him again.

CATEGORY: Inorganic construct

BASE OF OPERATIONS: Prague

WHEN: Every thirty-three years forever

MONSTROUS POWERS: It can grow bigger than you; it can paralyze you; perhaps it *is* you

WEAKNESS: Meth

MOST DASTARDLY DEEDS: Rabbi squishing

FEAR FACTOR: 💀💀💀💀

ASK YOURSELF: AM I A GOLEM?

There's an old joke that goes: "It's too late to run! The skeleton is already inside you." It might be too late to run from the Golem, is all I'm saying.

Until one Friday evening, when the rabbi forgot to deactivate the Golem. By Saturday the figure was taller than ever, and the rabbi could no longer reach its forehead! There was no way to rub out the "truth." There was no way to stop it from growing. Day after day it grew larger and larger.

Finally, the rabbi had an idea. He asked the Golem to tie his shoes for him. When the Golem bent over to tie the rabbi's shoes, the rabbi quickly wiped out the beginning of *'emeth*. Reduced once more to lifeless clay, the Golem toppled over—but its massive body crushed the rabbi in the process.

That was a long time ago. No one has been foolish enough to make a Golem since. But that doesn't mean the Golem was never seen again . . .

Before the rabbi could form the Golem out of clay, he had to form a Golem in his mind, imagining the shape his creation would take, as any sculptor would. Although the Golem of clay was destroyed, the Golem of the mind lived on. It appeared every thirty-three years in a certain room in Prague—a room with one barred window.

If the room had any doors, they must have been secret: No one in Prague knew how to get into the room. It was too high up to climb. Once a man tried lowering himself by rope from the top of the building, but the rope snapped, and that was the end of him.

But there must have been a way out of the room, for the Golem always managed to escape and wander the streets of Prague, dressed in an outlandishly old costume. Those who beheld him suffered a strange paralysis. It was as though they were looking not at a man of clay but at their own souls, staring back at them. Whenever the Golem showed up, Prague erupted in violence. There were murders. There were strange and sinister happenings.

Then, one dark night in the late nineteenth century, a jeweler named Athanasius Pernath accidentally stumbled upon a secret labyrinth of twisting tunnels and trap doors that led him to a room with one barred window. He looked out the window at the street below and passersby were terrified. They said that the Golem had returned.

Pernath's neighbor, Rabbi Hillel, said he didn't believe in the Golem. He said he wouldn't believe in it even if it was standing in front of him. And when he said this, he looked directly at Athanasius Pernath.

Pernath was a strange man who often could not distinguish his dreams from his life and who had almost no memories. Was Pernath the Golem? Was the Golem Pernath? Perhaps in thirty-three years, when the Golem returns, all will finally be made clear . . .

BEYOND THE BOOK

MODERNISM

The beginning of the twentieth century was marked by the rise of the artistic movement known as modernism. Modernist artists experimented with new ways of creating art—paintings that didn't look realistic, poetry that didn't rhyme or have a regular meter, novels that might not have a plot or characters or a setting.

Some modernist authors wrote in what's called "stream of consciousness," a jumbled tangle of words that depicts the subjective experiences inside a character's head. Rather than just reporting what happens to the character, they write about how the character perceives and understands what happens to them.

The Golem is written from the point of view of a character that doesn't always know what's going on. He doesn't even know who he is! This can make the book hard to understand, but as the writer Lionel Trilling once said about modernists, "We like difficult books."

THE OTHER WEIRD WRITER FROM PRAGUE

Gustav Meyrink was well known in his day, but his reputation has since been overshadowed by an even greater and even weirder author who wrote in Prague in the 1910s and 1920s: Franz Kafka.

Kafka's most famous monster is a salesman named Gregor Samsa, who wakes up one morning in bed in the form of an enormous insect. His family locks him in his room and complains about him. No one wants a giant insect in the family.

The Metamorphosis (1915), which chronicles Gregor's life in that little room, climbing up and down the walls on his gigantic spindly legs, is one of the saddest stories ever written.

HOW TO BUILD AN INORGANIC CONSTRUCT

The Golem is made of clay, but you can also make constructs out of:

- Bronze, in the *Argonautica* by Apollonius of Rhodes (ca. 250 BC). The Argonauts are a dream team of Greek mythological heroes who go on an epic quest to find the Golden Fleece. Along the way, they face many dangers—including the giant Talos. The Argonauts' weapons are worthless against him, for Talos is "fashioned of bronze and invulnerable." Fortunately for the heroes, they have the sorceress Medea on their side, and she deduces the giant's weak spot (his ankle), and uses her magic against him. "With a mighty thud" Talos falls.

- Brass, in *Friar Bacon and Friar Bungay* by Robert Greene (ca. 1590). The magician Roger Bacon constructs a head made of brass that can "unfold strange doubts and aphorisms, and read a lecture in philosophy." He plans to use the head to help him surround all of England with a defensive wall, also made of brass. Unfortunately, the head speaks only seven mysterious words—"Time is. Time was. Time is past"—before a phantom hand with a phantom hammer smashes the head to pieces.

- Futuristic chemical compounds, in *R.U.R.* by Karel Čapek (1921). This Czech drama is the source for our word *robot*—R.U.R stands for Rossum's Universal Robots, and *robota* in Czech means "forced labor." The play depicts a world in which robots are forced to toil for humanity . . . until, predictably, they rise up and exterminate us. Oops.

GRENDEL

FROM

BEOWULF

(8TH CENTURY)

Grendel had a lot of problems. He was descended from Cain, history's first murderer. He was brother to "evil things" such as "giants and elves and monsters of the deep." He disliked loud noises. And he lived with his mother underwater in a swamp.

When Hrothgar, the king of Denmark, built a great hall called Heorot, Grendel would pass nearby, and "daily he heard loud joy in the hall." People were laughing and feasting. "There was sound of harping, and the clear song of the bard." All the loud noises made Grendel furious. So at night, when everyone was sleeping, he snuck into Heorot, ate thirty Danes, and then ran home to "the moors among the misty hill-slopes." The next night, he came back for more.

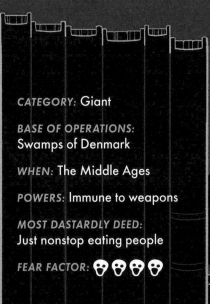

CATEGORY: Giant

BASE OF OPERATIONS:
Swamps of Denmark

WHEN: The Middle Ages

POWERS: Immune to weapons

MOST DASTARDLY DEED:
Just nonstop eating people

FEAR FACTOR: 💀💀💀💀

Now the Danes were Vikings and valiant warriors, and hardly people to sit around and get eaten passively. "Drunken with beer the warriors full often boasted o'er the ale-cup that they would bide in the beer-hall the battle of Grendel with the terror of swords." But what the Danes did not know was that Grendel's skin was invulnerable against "all victorious weapons and swords." When they tried to fight Grendel, their weapons bounced off the beast harmlessly, and soon the mead-hall was "all bloodstained, and all the benches were wet with gore."

Grendel had done his work once again.

Heorot was a beautiful hall, "the best of all houses," but anyone who tried to live in it died. For twelve years the Danes lived in fear. For twelve years Grendel "ruled and strove against right, he alone against all of them." A Dane for breakfast. A Dane for supper. A Dane for a midnight snack. Grendel was having a good time.

And then a man named Beowulf showed up to ruin his fun.

Beowulf was the "strongest of men in strength." He had made a name for himself purging the North Sea of sea monsters, and now he had come to Denmark to save Heorot from Grendel. "Don't worry, I got this," said Beowulf. (Actually, what he said was: "And now all alone I shall settle the affair of Grendel.")

That night, Beowulf and his men lay down in Heorot and pretended to sleep. Soon enough, Grendel came and, "in his fury," tore the hall door off its hinges. Before anyone could stop him, he grabbed a man "and tore him to pieces all unawares, and bit at the flesh and drank the streaming blood, and devoured huge pieces of flesh." And then the beast turned to Beowulf.

Now Beowulf knew that weapons just bounced off Grendel, so he vowed he would "forgo to carry to the battle a sword." Instead, he was going to wrestle.

As Grendel approached, Beowulf grabbed the monster's arms. Grendel "never had met in all the quarters of the earth amongst other men a greater hand-grip." The two strove for a moment, and then Beowulf squeezed hard. Grendel felt "his fingers burst." He tried to pull away, but Beowulf would not let go of his arm.

Grendel pulled harder, and a "gaping wound was seen on his shoulder. His sinews sprang open; and the bone-lockers burst." His arm was torn right off, but he was free. With Beowulf still holding his arm, Grendel fled Heorot and returned to his underwater lair. He told his mother what had happened to him. Then he lay down and died. "And hell received him."

Naturally, Grendel's mother wanted revenge. She came back to Heorot and started killing people, just like her son. Beowulf had to pursue her back to her swamp, where he finally slew her and freed Heorot from her terror.

Years later, in an unrelated incident, Beowulf was killed by a dragon.

BEYOND THE BOOK

BATTLE-SWEAT

Beowulf wielded a sword named Hrunting, "one of the ancient treasures. Its edge was of iron, and poison-tipped, and hardened in battle-sweat."

It sounds pretty cool, but . . . how could a sword be "hardened in battle-sweat"? What is battle-sweat, anyway?

"Battle-sweat" is a kind of metaphor called a *kenning*—a paraphrase that describes a common object in a roundabout, poetic way. "Battle-sweat" is blood, so Hrunting was tempered by plunging it in blood.

Some kennings in *Beowulf* are straightforward—"helmet-bearer" for a warrior, for instance—but others get more fanciful. The sea is the "whale-road," and when Beowulf gives a speech, he unlocks his "word-hoard." The name *Beowulf* is itself a kenning. It means "bee-wolf," or the beast that preys on bees like a wolf. Beowulf is named after a bear.

A modern kenning: *Skyscraper.*

OLD ENGLISH RIDDLES

Q: If you cut me, you are the one who cries. What am I?

A: An onion

Q: I have one eye, two ears, and a hundred heads. What am I?

A: A one-eyed onion salesman

There are lots of other riddles in Old English, but these are the only ones that are about onions.

OLD ENGLISH

Old English was the language spoken in England before the year 1066, when French speakers came in and changed everything. In Old English nouns have genders, like in French or Spanish. They also have multiple cases, as in Latin. Even the alphabet is different: Old English has extra letters, such as þ and ð (they both make a *th* sound).

Old English poetry like *Beowulf* doesn't rhyme. Instead, the poems use *alliteration*, which is when the starting sounds of syllables are the same (like that!). Each line of an Old English poem is divided into two halves, and one or more words from the first half of a line must alliterate with the same sound as one of the words in the second half of a line.

This is the opening of "Cædmon's Hymn," the oldest poem in English and one of the most famous examples of Old English poetry. The poem came to an illiterate English cowherd in a dream:

> *Nu we sculon herigean*   *heofonrices weard,*
>
>   *(Now we shall praise*   *heaven's warden,)*
>
> *Meotodes meahte*   *ond his modgeþanc . . .*
>
>   *(The creator's might*   *and his purpose . . .)*

The alliteration doesn't quite make it into the translation.

Although Old English looks weird, there are plenty of common English words—*finger, gold, storm, stream, dead*—that are spelled the same now as they were a thousand years ago. Other words are very close, like *wæter* or *bord*. The most common English words tend to come from Old English, and you can often spot a familiar word hiding inside a strange Old English one. A *treow* is a tree. A *cicen* is a chicken. A *hræfn* is a raven.

CYNEWULF

Most Old English poems, including *Beowulf*, are anonymous. There was no tradition at the time of writing "by so-and-so" at the top of a poem.

But one poet of the ninth century managed to find a secret way of signing his poems. Cynewulf hid his name in his poetry by using *runes*—letters that were used in Britain before our current alphabet caught on.

Runic letters had names that were also words—*feoh* meant "wealth," and the letter *f*, *wynn* meant "joy" and the letter *w*, and so on—and so Cynewulf cunningly substituted runes for select words in his poems. Put together, the runes spelled his name.

THE HEADLESS HORSEMAN

FROM "THE LEGEND OF SLEEPY HOLLOW"

BY WASHINGTON IRVING (1820)

The superstitious people of New York's Hudson Valley spoke of many ghosts, but the "commander-in-chief of all the powers of the air" around there was the most feared spirit in all of New York state the ghost of a Hessian from the American Revolution.

The Hessians were German soldiers hired by the British, and you may recognize them from the Declaration of Independence, which complains of "Armies of foreign Mercenaries" sent "to compleat the works of death, desolation and tyranny." This particular Hessian, though, did not "compleat" anything. A stray Patriot cannonball removed his head in battle, and his ghost began riding through the forests near Tarrytown

CATEGORY: Undead

BASE OF OPERATIONS: Tarrytown, New York

WHEN: Late 18th century

POWERS: Acephalous equestrianism (riding a horse while headless)

WEAKNESS: Reality

MOST DASTARDLY DEED: Head hucking

FEAR FACTOR: 💀💀

"in nightly quest of his head." They called him the Headless Horseman of Sleepy Hollow.

And who should blunder upon that headless fiend one fateful night but Ichabod Crane?

Crane was a superstitious, gossipy schoolteacher who had been living a peaceful life in Sleepy Hollow, New York, which was, after all, "one of the quietest places in the whole world."

Now, Ichabod already had a problem: He had fallen in love with a local heiress named Katrina Van Tassel, and Katrina was also being wooed by a man named Abraham "Brom Bones" Van Brunt.

Brom Bones was everything Ichabod was not. While Ichabod Crane looked like a "scarecrow eloped from a cornfield," Brom Bones was a titan of strength, "broad-shouldered and double-jointed." Ichabod was scared of spooks and goblins and "terrors of the night," while spirits were just a joke to Brom Bones. Most everything was a joke to Brom Bones, and the only thing

he loved more than a "rustic brawl" was a "madcap prank." So when Katrina started to favor meek Ichabod Crane, Brom Bones vowed to do something about it.

Not get her flowers. Not start acting like a decent upstanding citizen. That was not Brom Bones's way.

On the night of a party at the Van Tassels' home, the guests stayed up late swapping ghost stories—stories "about funeral trains, and mourning cries and

wailings heard" near the "enormous tulip-tree" where the British spy Major John André was captured, stories about a mysterious "woman in white" of Raven Rock who was "often heard to shriek on winter nights before a storm, having perished there in the snow," and especially stories about a galloping figure with no head. It was midnight—"the very witching time of night"— before Ichabod Crane mounted his horse and left for home.

Never before had the woods seemed so filled with terrors and hauntings for poor Ichabod. He was a superstitious man, and to a good imagination the dark woods on a dark night were filled with creaks and moans and half-glimpsed "ghosts and goblins." And then one figure, which Ichabod saw plainly. The figure of a man, "muffled in a cloak," riding a black horse.

It would not be accurate to say that the figure had no head. But, the head was not on his shoulders, where it should have been. Better to say that the figure had a head, and he carried it in his hand.

Well, that was about enough for Ichabod Crane! He rode away in terror, but the Headless Horseman followed him. The chase proceeded through the woods, and Ichabod strove to reach a bridge near a church where (legend says) the Hessian ghost would always disappear. Far from disappearing, though, when the Horseman reached the bridge, he threw his head at Ichabod, knocking him from his horse.

Ichabod took to his feet and didn't stop running until he reached Connecticut. He forgot all about Katrina Van Tassel, and he was never seen near Tarrytown again. The townsfolk decided "that Ichabod had been carried off by the Galloping Hessian."

It was not the Hessian that chased Ichabod to a neighboring state, however. The rider that pursued him was none other than Brom Bones, his face concealed inside his cloak, a pumpkin done up to look like a severed head. It was only a pumpkin he threw at poor Ichabod Crane.

Brom Bones married Katrina Van Tassel and presumably spent the rest of his life acting like a giant jerk. But he kept his secret and never confessed to his one-night role as the Headless Horseman.

Who was never seen riding again.

BEYOND THE BOOK

WHAT'S ON ICHABOD'S SHELF?

Washington Irving, with dry wit, notes that Ichabod Crane was "esteemed by the women as a man of great erudition, for he had read several books quite through." But when people search his house, they only find three:

- Cotton Mather's **History of New England Witchcraft**. Cotton Mather was a famous seventeenth-century Puritan preacher who popularized the Salem witch trials. He never wrote a book with this title, although he certainly wrote some books on similar topics, including *The Wonders of the Invisible World* (1693).

- **A New England almanac.** Almanacs were very popular in eighteenth- and nineteenth-century America, serving as calendars, weather predictors, and even clocks: The hours of sunrise and sunset every day gave many people their only clue as to what time it was. Almanacs of the day also included short stories, jokes, and poems.

- **"A book of dreams and fortune-telling."** This is pretty dumb. As far as "great erudition" goes, you're better off swapping books with Frankenstein's monster (see p. 52).

"SCOOBY-DOO" ENDINGS

In *Scooby-Doo* cartoons, the ghost often turns out to be some guy in a mask looking to scare people. This plot structure is taken directly from early Gothic stories, many of which set up a supernatural situation only to reveal later that the whole thing was a trick.

Ann Radcliffe may have invented this plot point. In *The Mysteries of Udolpho* (1794), the ghosts that terrify the characters are hoaxes made by pirates who "tried to have it believed that the chateau was haunted," so no one would find the loot they hid there.

Sometimes the ghost is just a misunderstanding. In Thomas Love Peacock's *Nightmare Abbey* (1818), "a ghastly figure, shrouded in white drapery, with the semblance of a bloody turban on its head" that terrorizes the abbey turns out to be the steward walking in his sleep. "The shroud and bloody turban were a sheet and a red nightcap."

THE HORLA

FROM

"THE HORLA"

BY GUY DE MAUPASSANT (1887)

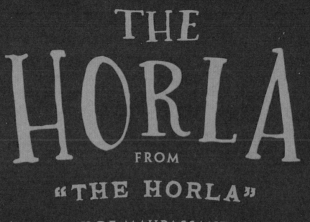

"There are only a few—so few—stages of development in this world, from the oyster up to man. Why should there not be one more?" And look! There is one more. As man is to the dumb beasts, so is the Horla to man. "A new being!"

The Horla began its dreadful business in Brazil, near São Paolo, herding people like "human cattle" and feeding "on their life" as they slept. First it made its victims listless and weak. Then it wormed its way into their brains so that they could not flee from it, even if they knew it was there. And they may not have known it was there, for mere human senses cannot perceive the Horla. It is completely invisible.

CATEGORY: ???

BASE OF OPERATIONS: From Brazil to France

WHEN: 1880s

POWERS: Invisibility; mind control

MOST DASTARDLY DEED: Treating humans like farm animals

FEAR FACTOR: 💀💀💀💀💀

As the Horla wreaked havoc in Brazil, it didn't look good for humanity. Inevitably, the Horla would "make of man what man has made of the horse and of the ox: his chattel, his slave, and his food, by the mere power of his will. Woe to us!"

Eventually, the Horla grew bored of Brazil and hopped a "magnificent Brazilian three-master" sailing to France. The stowaway jumped ship near the city of Rouen and chose a new victim, a nameless Frenchman.

Day by day the Frenchman chronicled his decline in his diary. First he was haunted by "the apprehension of some coming misfortune or of approaching death, a presentiment which is no doubt, an attack of some illness still unnamed." The symptoms were terrible: a "feverish enervation," an "incomprehensible feeling of disquietude" that came on as night closed in.

"Whence come those mysterious influences, which change our happiness into discouragement, and our self-confidence into diffidence?" he wrote. "One might almost say that the air, the invisible air, is full of unknowable Forces, whose mysterious presence we have to endure."

Plus, some strange things were happening. The Frenchman kept a decanter of water in his bedroom, and he awoke one morning to find the decanter empty, although he had no memory of getting out of bed or drinking it. Had he been sleepwalking?

As a test, he wrapped a water bottle in "white muslin" and tied down the stopper with knotted string. He covered his face and hands with "pencil lead" before he retired. When he woke up, there were no pencil marks on the muslin. The string still held the stopper in place. And yet the water was gone. Something had been drinking the water without opening the bottle.

There was a Horla in the house.

The Frenchman dreaded the night. He dreaded his bed. He steeled himself to "wait for sleep as a man might wait for the executioner." In his diary he wrote, "I am lost! Somebody possesses my soul and governs it! Somebody orders all my acts, all my movements, all my thoughts. I am no longer anything in myself, nothing except an enslaved and terrified spectator of all the things which I do. I wish to go out; I cannot. He does not wish to, and so I remain, trembling and distracted in the armchair in which he keeps me sitting. I merely wish to get up and to rouse myself, so as to think that I am still master of myself: I cannot! I am riveted to my chair."

Night by night, the Horla fed on him. Only for brief moments would its power slip. Once, when the Horla loosened its grip, the Frenchman fled the house, but before he could get to a railroad station and speed away to safety, the Horla reasserted itself. Meekly, the man returned home like the sheep that he was.

But the Frenchman was resilient. The next time the will of the Horla slipped, he called a locksmith and had iron shutters put on his bedroom windows. An innocent activity! The Horla didn't even bother to stop it.

THE HORLA'S REVENGE

The anonymous narrator of "The Horla" slowly goes mad under the creature's malign influence. Well, author Guy de Maupassant also slowly went mad. Four years after "The Horla" came out, Maupassant found himself in an insane asylum. He died there eighteen months later. There's your twist ending!

The Frenchman waited until he was certain the Horla was in his room, and then he slipped out, closing the door behind him and locking it with two padlocks.

The Horla was trapped. And before it could seize his will again, the Frenchman set his house on fire. From "a clump of laurel bushes" in the garden he watched his house tumble down in blazing shambles.

Surely he had killed the Horla! But then he worried. The Horla was so different from us that our feeble eyes could not perceive it. What if it was so different that fire could not harm it?

What if nothing could stop the Horla?

"The reign of man is over, and he has come."

BEYOND THE BOOK

HUMANS ARE ANIMALS

he Horla is not the only one who tries to domesticate humans. In Jonathan Swift's *Gulliver's Travels* (1726), the intrepid voyager Lemuel Gulliver journeys to the land of the Houyhnhnms—intelligent, civilized horses who use savage humans called Yahoos as beasts of burden. The Houyhnhnms are amazed by Gulliver, a lowly human who can nevertheless "imitate a rational creature." The only humans they've ever met have been good for nothing but pulling plows or carriages.

Over time, Gulliver comes to idolize the "wise and virtuous" Houyhnhnm horses and despise humanity. When he sails away from the land of the Houyhnhnms, it is in a boat made from the "skins of Yahoos"—that is to say, of humans.

WEIRD TALES

"he Horla" was very influential on a particular kind of fiction sometimes called "weird tales." The writer H. P. Lovecraft, in his essay "Supernatural Horror in Literature" (1927), says that weird tales should give "the reader a profound sense of dread, and of contact with unknown spheres and powers" from "the known universe's utmost rim."

Lovecraft singles out for praise *The Golem* (see p. 60) for "its haunting shadowy suggestions of marvels and horrors just beyond reach," as well as the works of Edgar Allan Poe, *Frankenstein*, and especially "The Horla" as a story "perhaps without a peer."

Of course, if "the true weird tale" must possess "breathless and unexplainable dread of outer, unknown forces," as Lovecraft claims, then the true master of the weird tale is Lovecraft himself. In a series of stories, starting with "The Call of Cthulhu" (1928), Lovecraft produced terrifying narratives of ancient gods and extra-planetary beings of immense power who care nothing for humanity, and constantly threaten to crush us like ants.

HUMBABA

FROM

THE EPIC OF GILGAMESH

(CA. 1750 BC)

In the oldest days, Lebanon was famous for its forests of massive cedar trees. The ancient Phoenicians used these trees to build their fleets. King Solomon of Israel used these trees to build his temple.

The Mesopotamian god Enlil, "in order that the cedar wood remain intact," created a guardian, "a terror for the people." Who guarded the cedars of Lebanon? Humbaba, "whose roar is a flood, whose mouth is fire, whose breath is death." His face was like a lion's, but it was covered in blood, and his mouth had sharp teeth and tusks sticking straight out.

For eons, Humbaba kept watch over Lebanon's wild forests. Until the day Gilgamesh and Enkidu came along.

CATEGORY: Demigod

BASE OF OPERATIONS: Lebanon

WHEN: 4,500 years ago

POWERS: Breathing fire; changing faces; death breath

MOST DASTARDLY DEED: Gilgamesh swears he's evil, but mostly Humbaba just guards the forest.

FEAR FACTOR: 💀💀💀💀

Gilgamesh and Enkidu were a pair of buddy adventurers. Gilgamesh, king of Uruk, was one-third man and two-thirds god, which is a difficult combination to achieve. Enkidu was his best friend, a savage wild man whose "whole body was covered with hair." Enkidu had grown up in the wilderness, where "he ate herbs with the gazelles" and "quenched his thirst with the beasts." They were the two strongest men in the world, and when the gods sent the Bull of Heaven to toss them around and teach them a lesson, they just killed it.

Now they were looking to slay Humbaba—perhaps because Gilgamesh was a hero, and heroes slay monsters, or perhaps just because Gilgamesh wanted some cedars to build a temple.

Enkidu, who used to live in the forest and had seen Humbaba at a distance, counseled against the attack. This was Humbaba, "the terrible one." He knew everything that happened in his forest, and he could hear even the slightest shifting of a leaf. Better not to enter the cedar forests and die. Better to stay in Uruk. But if people could talk Gilgamesh out of anything, he wouldn't have killed the Bull of Heaven.

"HUMBABA IS AS VIOLENT AS THE ONCOMING STORM; LIKE THE GOD OF STORMS, HE WILL DESTROY US."

—ENKIDU

Gilgamesh was heading for Humbaba's lair, and Enkidu was not about to let him go alone. Together they ventured to the forest, and "astonished they gazed at the height of the cedars and at the entrance of the cedar wood, where Humbaba was wont to walk with lofty steps."

And together they entered.

Three times, over three nights, Gilgamesh dreamed strange and terrifying dreams in that forest. Enkidu interpreted the dreams and told Gilgamesh that he would be fine. But Enkidu himself only grew more and more afraid.

Then Humbaba showed up. His face was just as terrifying as Enkidu had remembered it, but what was worse, as they watched, "his face was changed" into horrible visage after horrible visage, a catalog of nightmares. In a voice "like that of a storm cyclone," he spoke "like a hot wind," vowing that he would kill the heroes and feed their corpses to the birds of his forest.

Humbaba was fierce, but no one could stand before the combined might of Gilgamesh and Enkidu, not in the old Sumerian days. They battered

Humbaba down, and when he begged for his life, Enkidu, who knew that the guardian of the forest spoke in lies and tricks, told Gilgamesh not to listen.

Just before Gilgamesh chopped his head off with his great ax, Humbaba uttered a curse: One day Enkidu would die, and Gilgamesh would be humbled by his grief.

Then they chopped off Humbaba's head anyway, and they dismembered him, and they cut down his cedars to build things with.

But Humbaba got his revenge. Not that Enkidu died right away. He and Gilgamesh had more adventures, but everything they did seemed to anger one god or another. Finally, the gods had had enough. They decided that it was time for Humbaba's curse to strike home. One night, Enkidu dreamed he was dying, and when he woke up, he was.

Gilgamesh wept for his friend. But then he realized something for the first time: that someday, he would die, too. Instead of weeping for Enkidu, Gilgamesh started weeping for Gilgamesh.

Being a hero, Gilgamesh did not merely bemoan his fate. He decided to do something about it. He decided to go in search of the secret of immortality, the quest that takes up the second half of the *Epic of Gilgamesh*.

VALENTINE & ORSON

The relationship between Gilgamesh and Enkidu—buddy heroes, one civilized and one savage—has an echo in the medieval legends of Charlemagne's knights.

Two of Charlemagne's paladins were twins named Valentine and Orson. They were separated at birth—Valentine was raised by a king, while Orson was raised by bears. As adults, they met, teamed up, and fought evil knights and rampaging lions all across eighth-century France.

BEYOND THE BOOK

THE OLDEST STORY IN THE WORLD?

The Epic of Gilgamesh isn't quite the oldest story in the world, but it's the oldest *really good* story in the world—at least the oldest one that survives to this day. It was a popular work for a thousand years, appearing throughout the Middle East in different versions and different translations—and then it was forgotten. For two thousand years, no one heard of Gilgamesh or Enkidu.

But the clay tablets the epic was written on were preserved in the dry climate of Mesopotamia. In 1853, archaeologists turned up a fragment of the epic. Over time, more and more versions showed up, all of them fragmentary—but by comparing and combining them, we can read an almost-complete version of the story.

STRANGE CREATURES OF MESOPOTAMIA

The ruined buildings of ancient Mesopotamia in the Middle East are filled with statues of strange creatures that look like winged bulls but with bearded human heads. Sometimes they are carved with five legs, three in the front and two in the back. Called *lammasu* or *shedu*, these statues frequently flank gates and doorways.

Other ancient Mesopotamian monsters include *Imdugud* (a cross between a lion and an eagle) and the terrible retinue of the primordial dragon Tiamat, which includes "the Whirlwind, the ravening Dog, the Scorpion-man, the mighty Storm-wind, the Fish-man, and the Horned Beast" (as listed in E. A. Wallis Budge's *The Babylonian Legends of Creation and the Fight Between Bel and the Dragon*, 1921).

MR. HYDE

FROM

THE STRANGE CASE OF DR. JEKYLL AND MR. HYDE

BY ROBERT LOUIS STEVENSON (1886)

Dr. Henry Jekyll was a good man. He was a successful man. He held degrees in law and medicine. He was a member of the Royal Society, an organization for promoting scientific knowledge. He was active in his church. He had "always been known for charities." A very good man indeed!

But there was a problem. Jekyll had a wild streak, and he was "guilty" of "irregularities." What did he do, exactly? Gamble? Drink? Run around with the ladies? Jekyll never made clear what his "irregularities" were. He was too ashamed! But not ashamed enough to stop.

What do you do if you're a good man who wants to do bad things?

CATEGORY: Science experiment

BASE OF OPERATIONS: London

WHEN: 1880s

POWERS: Shape-shifting

WEAKNESS: Running out of drugs

MOST DASTARDLY DEED: Serial trampling

FEAR FACTOR: 💀💀💀

Dr. Jekyll spent ten years working on a solution to this very problem. He created a chemical compound that he could drink to free the "lower elements" of his nature. When he consumed the compound, Dr. Jekyll, that good man, temporarily disappeared and was replaced by one Edward Hyde.

Dr. Henry Jekyll was a good man. Edward Hyde was not.

"EDWARD HYDE, ALONE IN THE RANKS OF MANKIND, WAS PURE EVIL."

This "particularly small and particularly wicked-looking" man could do things that Jekyll would never dare to do. Whatever vices Jekyll craved, Hyde indulged in—and Jekyll, when he returned, felt no shame. Don't look at me! It was Hyde!

For a while, Jekyll and Hyde were happy.

But you shouldn't give your "evil side" flesh if you want it to behave well. Behaving well is not what evil sides are good at. Before long, Mr. Hyde began indulging in "monstrous" behavior. Soon, he had "trampled" a little girl he encountered in the street. She wasn't too badly hurt—Hyde was too small to be a very effective trampler. But he was bound to try again.

And he was getting stronger. He was growing larger. One day, Dr. Jekyll went to sleep and woke up as Mr. Hyde, no potion needed. Hyde was getting out of control.

Then, late one night, Hyde encountered a certain Sir Danvers Carew, an elderly man out to post a letter. Immediately, "with ape-like fury," Hyde leaped upon Carew and began "trampling his victim under foot." Worse yet, he beat Carew to death with his cane.

When Hyde transformed back into Jekyll, the good doctor was naturally horrified. But his conscience was clear! "It was Hyde, after all, and Hyde alone, that was guilty," Jekyll said. Still, he

WHAT DOES MR. HYDE LOOK LIKE?

No one can say! "He is not easy to describe," one witness testifies. "There is something wrong with his appearance; something displeasing, something downright detestable. I never saw a man I so disliked, and yet I scarce know why."

Another says, "God bless me, the man seems hardly human! Something troglodytic, shall we say?" (A troglodyte is a cave dweller.)

vowed to keep Hyde locked up inside him, and let his evil side out no more. That way there would be no more murders.

But it was too late. Jekyll was turning into Hyde now without the potion.

In fact, the only way Jekyll could stay Jekyll was with the constant application of this medicine. Worse yet, the potion was running out, and Jekyll was having a hard time mixing up more.

Hyde grew more and more dominant—but he was a trapped man. If he went outside, he'd be sent to the gallows for the murder of Sir Danvers Carew! So he spent his time doing the only thing he knew how to do—being a jerk—to the only person around—Dr. Jekyll. When Jekyll would

take over for brief periods of time, he'd find that Hyde had wrecked his stuff and scrawled "blasphemies" all over his books.

Jekyll knew that soon there would be only Hyde. In despair, before Hyde could stop him, Jekyll took his own life. His friends found him in the lab, dead. Next to him was a confession that Hyde never had the chance to destroy.

BEYOND THE BOOK

JEKYLL VS. VAN HELSING

If Henry Jekyll and Abraham Van Helsing (from *Dracula*—see page 32) competed to see who had more degrees, honors, and letters after their name, who would win?

Jekyll: "M.D., D.C.L., L.L.D., F.R.S., etc."

Van Helsing: "M.D., D.Ph., D.Lit., etc., etc."

As we can see, Jekyll has four to Van Helsing's three, but Van Helsing has two etceteras to Jekyll's one, so he may have more that he was just too modest to mention.

A REVIEW FROM PRISON

In 1911, the *New York Times* published a series of book reviews of classic literature they found in the Sing Sing prison library. An anonymous convict penned the reviews. See if you can follow the antiquated slang in his review of Jekyll and Hyde:

"This one is a hair-raiser. It'll give you the horrors in a jiffy. The Doc. has wheels in his sky-piece; he butts into some kind of hop that brings out all that's bum in him; changes him into a Mr. Hyde who goes out and plays the scoundrel, then changes him back into the genial Doc. again. In the end he loses the combination to his hop and has to shuffle off this mortal coil as Mr. Hyde. We got so sore at him we'd like to have been able to hand him a few swift swats in the breadbasket."

A sky-piece is a hat, but here it probably means "brain." Hop is a drug. The breadbasket is the belly.

THE INVISIBLE MAN

FROM

THE INVISIBLE MAN

BY H. G. WELLS (1897)

Before there was an Invisible Man, there was a Visible Man. His name was Griffin, and he was a bright young college student specializing in medicine and physics—especially optics, the study of light. His great discovery was a method for making living tissue invisible.

At first it was just a theory, and like any good scientist, Griffin knew his theory had to be tested. And so he swiped his neighbor's white cat.

This is how you make a cat invisible: First you sedate the cat (or it won't sit still). Then you give it injections to "decolorize" its red blood. After that you place the cat between two vibrating dynamos that change the cat's body so it no longer reflects light.

CATEGORY: Science experiment

BASE OF OPERATIONS: South of England

WHEN: 1890s

MOST DASTARDLY DEEDS: Murder; vandalism; kicking a dog

WEAKNESS: Footprints; winter

POWERS: Invisibility; extraordinary irascibility

FEAR FACTOR: 💀 💀 💀

Griffin powered up his dynamos and the white cat became as transparent as air, except for its claws and the section of its eyes called the tapetum lucidum—the part that makes cats' eyes shine at night.

This was all well and good until the cat woke up, justifiably annoyed, loudly meowing, and, what was worse, hard to catch. By the time Griffin shooed the invisible cat out the window, his landlord had accused him of torturing cats in his room and tried to evict him.

Since the cat experiment was a success, Griffin was ready to try the procedure on himself and enjoy "all the fantastic advantages an invisible man would have in the world." He fired up the dynamos, took off his clothes, and soon he was visible no more.

After setting fire to his apartment building to cover his tracks, the invisible Griffin began to roam the streets of London, prepared for a life of ease. But things did not go as planned.

First of all, London in January is no place to walk around naked, invisible or not. London is also crowded, and people kept stepping on toes they could not see. Invisible Griffin had thought he could steal whatever he needed, but he soon learned that he couldn't carry anything away without being noticed— imagine money or food floating away in midair, gripped in invisible hands.

"What a helpless absurdity an invisible man was—in a cold and dirty climate and a crowded civilised city."

So Griffin found himself living like an animal on the streets of London, caging scraps of food and sleeping in corners. He finally jumped the old proprietor of a costume shop, tied him up, and stole a wig and mask, along with some clothes. He left the old man bound and gagged. "I suppose he untied himself," Griffin guessed later. But he didn't give it much thought. There were more important people to worry about—like Griffin!

By now, poor Griffin had grown disillusioned with invisibility. Even with his mask and wig, he could hardly live a normal life—normal people don't walk around in masks. Finally, he decided to wind a bandage around his face, like a burn victim. He still looked unusual, but with gloves and a hat on, he didn't look like a monster.

In this disguise, Griffin traveled south to the sleepy little town of Iping and holed himself up in a local inn, vowing to make himself visible again and end this hellish existence.

The formula for re-visibility, alas, eluded him. Furthermore, as you may have noticed, Griffin could be unpleasant. He soon alienated the proprietress of the inn, as well as the locals. Also, he had a bad habit of leaving the door to his room open. Passersby who stuck their heads in risked a conk from a floating chair, swung by invisible arms. Or perhaps they'd see "a most singular thing, what seemed a handless arm waving"—the Invisible Man with his gloves off.

As experiment after experiment failed, Griffin took to throwing temper tantrums, smashing his test tubes, and cursing all through the night. He was a most difficult tenant. Also, he never paid his bills.

When a nearby house was burglarized, the townsfolk naturally suspected the most suspicious character in town. Griffin stripped naked to avoid the police, but Griffin being Griffin, he didn't escape until after he beat up the constable and anyone else he could reach. On his way out, he kicked a dog.

Griffin was now back to square one, naked and penniless. He passed the time "smiting and overthrowing, for the mere satisfaction of hurting." He broke a lot of windows. He beat an unfortunate man named Wicksteed to death with a piece of fence. He decided to begin a "reign of terror," killing anyone who disobeyed him.

In the coastal town of Port Burdock, Griffin declared himself the sovereign ruler. He was "Invisible Man the First." He also announced the man who would be executed first: Dr. Kemp, an old friend from medical school who happened to have a practice in town. Kemp had refused to assist Griffin in his murderous plans, and so he had to pay.

"THIS IS DAY ONE OF YEAR ONE OF THE NEW EPOCH— THE EPOCH OF THE INVISIBLE MAN."

Kemp ran away and Griffin pursued him, invisibly, until the two ran into a crowd. The crowd couldn't see Griffin, but they didn't need to. They had him surrounded. Griffin was one man against a multitude, and the multitude beat him to death.

As his lifeless body lay in the street, first his nerves, "then the glassy bones and intricate arteries, then the flesh and skin," became visible.

BEYOND THE BOOK

H. G. WELLS'S OTHER MONSTERS

Wells being Wells, he couldn't stop writing books full of monsters.

- *The Time Machine* (1895). A nameless time traveler visits the year AD 802,701 and encounters two species descended from humanity: the Eloi, a short, weak people who are friendly but as dumb as cattle; and the Morlocks, monstrous albino cannibals who can see in the dark. The Morlocks live beneath the earth's surface and only come up into the air on moonless nights . . . to seize and feast upon the gentle Eloi.

- **The Island of Dr. Moreau** (1896). A mad scientist on a remote island in the Pacific creates humanlike hybrids by surgically combining animals. There's a hyena-swine, a rhinoceros-horse, a bear-fox, a goat-ape, a leopard-man, and all sorts of other terrible mixtures. They can walk and speak like humans, but their animal natures are always threatening to come out. The question is whether these beast folk can make it to the end of the novel without eating flesh. (Spoiler: They can't.)

- **The War of the Worlds** (1898). "Unspeakably nasty" creatures have come from Mars to conquer Earth. They have disgusting "lipless" mouths that drool constantly. They have "gorgon groups of tentacles." All of that is bad enough, but they also have a "ghostly, terrible Heat-Ray" that roasts everyone in their path.

WELLS'S PLAN FOR PEACE

Wells was a peace activist, and he developed an unusual plan to end war, which he outlined in two books, *Floor Games* (1911) and *Little Wars* (1913). The idea was to get children interested in realistic war games with tin soldiers. By playing these "floor games" (you set the soldiers up on the floor), kids would learn the futility of war, and as adults would have no desire to engage in the bloody sport.

Unfortunately for Wells, the year after *Little Wars* came out, the world erupted into World War I, the largest war history had yet seen.

THE RING OF GYGES

Twenty-five hundred years ago, the Greek philosopher Plato wrote in the *Republic* a story that inspired *The Invisible Man*. In the story, a shepherd named Gyges discovers a magic ring that makes him invisible and finds himself able to do anything he wants. He can "kill or release from prison whom he would, and in all respects be like a God among men." So he kills the king and makes himself ruler of the land.

Plato's argument is that "no man can be imagined to be of such an iron nature that he would stand fast in justice" when he is tempted by a power like invisibility.

THE JABBERWOCK

FROM

THROUGH THE LOOKING-GLASS

BY LEWIS CARROLL (1871)

The Jabberwock has jaws that bite, claws that catch, and eyes of flame. It is manxome. It whiffles and burbles.

Alice found this useful information in a book on the other side of the looking glass (that's an old term for a mirror). She had previously explored Wonderland, and later passed through her mirror to the looking-glass realm. There she found a book—"in some language I don't know," she said—before she realized that it was simply English written in reverse. Holding the book to a mirror, Alice revealed the perfectly clear and simple poem.

CATEGORY: Whiffler

BASE OF OPERATIONS: Looking-Glass Land

WHEN: Brillig

POWERS: Manxomeness

WEAKNESS: Vorpality

MOST DASTARDLY DEED: Terrorizing the tulgey wood

FEAR FACTOR: 💀💀

JABBERWOCKY

'Twas brillig, and the slithy toves

Did gyre and gimble in the wabe;

All mimsy were the borogoves,

And the mome raths outgrabe.

"Beware the Jabberwock, my son!

The jaws that bite, the claws that catch!

Beware the Jubjub bird, and shun

The frumious Bandersnatch!"

He took his vorpal sword in hand:

Long time the manxome foe he sought—

So rested he by the Tumtum tree,

And stood awhile in thought.

And as in uffish thought he stood,

The Jabberwock, with eyes of flame,

Came whiffling through the tulgey wood,

And burbled as it came!

One, two! One, two! And through and through

The vorpal blade went snicker-snack!

He left it dead, and with its head

He went galumphing back.

"And hast thou slain the Jabberwock?

Come to my arms, my beamish boy!

O frabjous day! Callooh! Callay!"

He chortled in his joy.

Alice's verdict: "It seems very pretty, but it's rather hard to understand! Somehow it seems to fill my head with ideas—only I don't exactly know what they are! However, somebody killed something: that's clear, at any rate."

Later, Alice met Humpty Dumpty, and he explained some of the mysterious words in the poem. Some, he said, are like a portmanteau—a suitcase that opens into two parts—because "there are two meanings packed up into one word." *Slithy* is packed with "lithe" and "slimy." *Mimsy* is packed with "flimsy" and "miserable." These are portmanteau words. Others are harder to guess: *Brillig* is "four o'clock in the afternoon" and a *wabe* is a "grass-plot round a sun-dial."

These may seem like strange definitions, but Humpty Dumpty proclaimed, "When I use a word, it means just what I choose it to mean—neither more nor less." And once Humpty Dumpty has explained what a *tove* is, the rest of the poem makes perfect sense.

Doesn't it?

BEYOND THE BOOK

VICTORIAN NONSENSE

Lewis Carroll wrote nonsense verse—which means his poems aren't supposed to make sense. Nonsense verse became very popular during the Victorian era, when people began to fear that maybe it was the world that didn't make sense. The technological and social changes that would rock the twentieth century—advances in transportation, in communication, in women's rights—had just started when *Through the Looking-Glass* was published in 1871, but already people were feeling uneasy. As a result, Victorian nonsense poetry is often scary and dark.

While nonsense verse may not seem to hold any meaning on the surface, it's worth taking a closer look. Carroll's greatest nonsense poem is the long "The Hunting of the Snark" (1876), which looks like a funny nonsense epic about a Baker's quest for a mythical creature known as a Snark. But there's a danger: If the Snark happens to be a Boojum, the Baker "will softly and suddenly vanish away, and never be met with again."

There are many interpretations of "The Hunting of the Snark," but this is the usual one: The Snark is the true nature of reality. If the Snark is a Boojum, then life is meaningless. Through science and philosophy, we learn more and more about the world, but we're always in danger of learning too much and finding out that the world is a Boojum. Indeed, the poem ends with the Baker disintegrating—"for the Snark was a Boojum, you see."

THE GOSTAK DISTIMS THE DOSHES

In 1903, Andrew Ingraham wrote the sentence, "The gostak distims the doshes."

Philosophers have used Ingraham's sentence to talk about how we can understand the grammar of a sentence even when we don't know what the words mean. When we read that "slithy toves did gyre and gimble in the wabe," we know that *tove* and *wabe* are nouns, *gimble* and *gyre* are verbs, and *slithy* is an adjective. Familiar words like *the* and *did* help us figure this out.

And the greater the number of familiar words we see, the easier it is to puzzle out a strange word's meaning from context. *Manxome* has to mean "scary" or "tough," because it's describing a fiery-eyed monster. "O frabjous day!" can only be a cry of celebration, so whatever *frabjous* means, it must be something good.

If only we had a little more context, maybe we could figure out what a gostak is . . .

PHANTASMAGORIA

lthough his Alice books are his most famous, Lewis Carroll wrote other humorous novels and collections of poems for children. "Phantasmagoria" (1869) describes a lengthy argument between the narrator and the phantom that haunts his house (it's all a big misunderstanding). When the narrator tells the ghost not to be so shy, the ghost replies:

> "And as to being in a fright,
>   Allow me to remark
> That Ghosts have just as good a right
> In every way, to fear the light,
>   As Men to fear the dark."

THE LAMIA

FROM

"LAMIA"

BY JOHN KEATS (1820)

I magine a serpent "of dazzling hue," with crimson stripes "like a zebra," vermilion spots "like a pard" (a leopard), and a crest on her head that glows with a pale fire "sprinkled with stars." Now imagine that this snake has the mouth of a woman. Also, she can do magic.

This is the Lamia. She claims that she was once a woman but was turned into a snake by some mysterious process. She has a tendency to tell lies, though, so take her account with a grain of salt.

One of the Lamia's magic powers was the ability to spy on distant locations. Since life as a snake is pretty dull, she used to amuse herself when trapped "in the serpent prison-house" by taking in the sights all over Greece

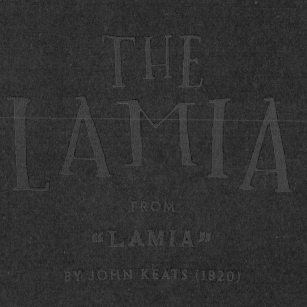

CATEGORY: Cursed human

BASE OF OPERATIONS: Greece

WHEN: "Upon a time"

POWERS: Teleportation, magic, shape-shifting

WEAKNESS: Hearing the truth

MOST DASTARDLY DEED:

One day, while spying far and wide, she happened to notice a handsome young Corinthian man named Lycius. She never forgot the sight, and as soon as she had abandoned her snake body, she teleported herself to Corinth and appeared before Lycius in the form of a beautiful woman. Lycius quickly fell in love and they decided to marry.

What did the Lamia want with a handsome young man? Perhaps she, too, was in love. But perhaps she was merely hungry.

It was easy for a magical woman to plan a wedding. The Lamia's "subtle servitors"—that is, her spells—decked the wedding hall in illusions of splendor. But there was a little problem: an uninvited guest.

In Corinth at that time there lived a man called Apollonius of Tyana, a "bald-head philosopher" and perhaps the wisest man in Greece. He had studied at Plato's Academy and learned that appearances are deceiving. The

Lamia had begged Lycius not to invite this philosopher to the wedding, but the old man crashed it anyway, and when he saw the bride, he was not fooled. His eye pierced her disguise "like a sharp spear." He asked the groom:

"SHALL I SEE THEE MADE A SERPENT'S PREY?"

Her power broken by hearing the truth, the Lamia vanished "with a frightful scream."

Lycius was not saved, though. He died immediately of a broken heart and was buried in his wedding clothes. Nice try, Apollonius.

That was all a long time ago. Whether the Lamia survived, whether she lives today, and what she's been doing all this time remain unknown. Presumably, if she still lives, she is once again in the bizarre form of a rainbow snake with a woman's mouth.

OTHER LAMIAS

Greek mythology tells many stories about a monster named Lamia, none of which quite match Keats's version. In one story, Lamia is a beautiful woman from Libya. She is beloved by Zeus, so Zeus's jealous wife Hera turns Lamia into a monster and curses her so that she can never sleep. Zeus cannot undo his wife's curse, but he gifts Lamia with the power of being able to remove her eyes from their sockets. When she wants to rest, she pops out her eyes and stores them in a cup.

BEYOND THE BOOK

ROMANTICISM!

John Keats was part of the artistic movement known as Romanticism. Romantics wrote about the power of the imagination! Deep emotions! Individual genius! Rebellion! Nature! These are all Romantic things.

Previous artistic movements had focused on moderation and balance, but Romantics liked extreme situations. Romantics were as happy brooding on windswept mountain crags or skulking through pestilential swamps as they were romping in fields of flowers.

When Keats describes the Lamia turning from a snake into a woman, for example, he is full of romantic notions:

> Her mouth foam'd, and the grass, therewith besprent [sprinkled],
> Wither'd at dew so sweet and virulent;
> Her eyes in torture fix'd, and anguish drear,
> Hot, glazed, and wide, with lid-lashes all sear,
> Flash'd phosphor and sharp sparks, without one cooling tear.

To recap: She drools poison that kills the grass beneath her, and the pain of the transformation is so great that her eyes shoot sparks of fire!

THE MOST ROMANTIC DEATH

Tuberculosis, which used to be called consumption, was a very Romantic disease. Romantic poets should die young, of course (dying young is very Romantic), and since tuberculosis was considered an artist's disease, the best way a young Romantic writer could die was from tuberculosis. John Keats did it (age twenty-five). Novalis did it (age twenty-eight). Emily Brontë did it (age thirty).

Lord Byron once said, "I should like to die of the consumption . . . because the ladies would all say, 'Look at that poor Byron, how interesting he looks in dying.'" But Byron died fighting to free Greece from the Ottoman Empire. It was a Romantic death, but it wasn't as good as tuberculosis.

THE LYNG GHOST

FROM

"AFTERWARD"

BY EDITH WHARTON (1910)

Every self-respecting old house in England has a ghost.

You might think, if you visit the dusty old house called Lyng in Dorset, that no ghost frequents its shadowy corridors. But Lyng does have a ghost, you just won't be aware of it. At least not "till long, long afterward." It's a ghost you only know about "in retrospect." It doesn't seem to make much sense, but as the locals say, "that's the story."

Consider the case of Ned and Mary Boyne, Americans who moved to Lyng after Ned had made his fortune in investments. Ned and Mary both loved ghost stories, and they eagerly awaited the day when they would see the ghost of

CATEGORY: Undead

BASE OF OPERATIONS: Dorset, England

WHEN: Some say the ghost is always there

POWERS: We won't know until afterward

MOST DASTARDLY DEED: No more Ned

FEAR FACTOR: 💀💀💀💀

Lyng—or rather, the day "afterward," when they would become aware that they had already seen it.

Lyng was very pleasant, and Dorset was beautiful. The only disappointment in the Boynes' lives was that day followed day, and the ghost they had hoped for never showed.

And then, one perfectly ordinary day, a stranger came to see Ned. Mary let him in. Soon after, Ned and the stranger walked out of the house. Neither was ever seen again.

The police searched the countryside. There was no body. There was no ransom note. There was no trace of Ned at all.

Afterward—long, long afterward—a lawyer came to see Mary. He explained that Ned had made his fortune by ripping off a man named Robert Elwell. Completely broke, Elwell had taken his own life some time before. The lawyer showed Mary a photo of Elwell, and Mary recognized him as the stranger that had come to see her husband.

But that was impossible! Elwell had died an ocean away. He was already dead the day the stranger came.

Then Mary understood the terrible nature of the ghost of Lyng. She cried in grief:

"OH MY GOD! I SENT HIM TO NED—I TOLD HIM WHERE TO GO!"

Elwell had come as a ghost and spirited Ned away. Mary had seen the ghost of Lyng after all, but she had not realized it.

Until afterward.

AN END TO THIS!

"I desire that you bring me no more stories of ghosts; for, though I do not believe in such things, yet, when one is awake in the night, one is apt, if one thinks of them, to have fancies that give one a kind of a chill, particularly if one opens one's eyes suddenly on one's dressing gown, hanging in the moonlight, between the bed and the window."

—From *Nightmare Abbey* by Thomas Love Peacock (1818)

BEYOND THE BOOK

THE GOTHIC HOUSE

Gothic fiction almost always takes place in an old, scary manor or decaying castle.

The term *gothic* actually comes from architecture. Horace Walpole chose to call *The Castle of Otranto* (1764) "a Gothic Story" because of the Gothic design of the medieval buildings that appear in the novel, with their stone gargoyles and stained-glass windows and fancy arches. The tale also features haunted castles with secret passages, family curses, and old portraits that seem to come to life—all hallmarks of Gothic fiction.

Thomas Love Peacock's *Nightmare Abbey* (1818) is "a venerable family mansion, in a highly picturesque state of semi-dilapidation" with "sliding panels and secret passages, that would have baffled the skill of the Parisian police." Jane Austen's *Northanger Abbey* (1818) is a "decayed" house "rich in Gothic ornaments" with "high Gothic windows" and "many gloomy passages."

The greatest spooky Gothic house, though, comes from Edgar Allan Poe's "Fall of the House of Usher" (1839). It is a "mansion of gloom" with "bleak walls," "vacant eye-like windows," and a "Gothic archway" leading to "many dark and intricate passages"—but what's inside is even more terrifying: Roderick Usher, a sickly man with a "ghastly pallor of the skin" and a "cadaverousness of complexion," and his sister Madeline, even more ghastly and cadaverous. In fact, she is so ghastly and cadaverous that she is mistaken for a corpse and buried alive.

GHOSTS IN SHAKESPEARE

William Shakespeare did not just write plays, he also acted in them—and one role that legend says he played onstage was the ghost of Hamlet's murdered father. This is Shakespeare's most famous ghost, but it's hardly the only ghost he ever wrote. There are also ghosts in:

- *Macbeth* (ca. 1606). After Macbeth has his friend Banquo murdered, Banquo's ghost shows up as Macbeth is about to eat dinner—and sits in Macbeth's chair! "The table's full," says Macbeth, surprised.

- *Julius Caesar* (ca. 1599). After Brutus kills Julius Caesar, great Caesar's ghost comes to visit him on the eve of battle. Caesar says he'll see Brutus at Philippi—and sure enough, Brutus goes to Philippi and dies.

- *Richard III* (ca. 1593). After King Richard kills, like, a lot of people—you see the pattern here—his victims' ghosts appear before him one night and tell him, one by one, to "despair, and die!" (Soon he does.)

HAMLET'S DEAD DAD

THE GHOST STORY THAT WASN'T

In 1898, Henry James released one of his most popular tales, *The Turn of the Screw*. It tells the spooky story of a governess who learns that ghosts are trying to claim the two children in her charge.

For thirty years, people read the story and got scared, as readers of ghost stories should. Nobody thought there was anything weird about it.

But in the 1930s, some readers, including the famous critic Edmund Wilson, started noticing unusual details. The only person who ever sees the ghosts is the governess. She narrates the whole story, and at times she sounds like she's lying—or crazy. What if there were no ghosts? What if the governess hallucinated the whole thing?

MEDUSA

FROM

THE METAMORPHOSES

BY OVID (8; LIKE THE YEAR AD 8!)

Pity poor Medusa! Once she was the toast of ancient Greece, admired above all for her elaborately done hair. Everyone noticed it—including Neptune, the god of the sea.

It was not safe for a mortal to be noticed by the gods, though, for the gods were cruel and pitiless. Neptune assaulted Medusa in the temple of the goddess Minerva.

Minerva, cruel and pitiless herself, was angry that her temple had been profaned. She wanted revenge, but it's hard to curse a god like Neptune. Instead, her vengeance fell on Medusa, who hadn't wanted to be there in the first place.

Minerva cursed Medusa with the deadliest curse any vengeful

CATEGORY: Cursed human

BASE OF OPERATIONS: Libya

WHEN: Way back, before the Trojan War

POWERS: Hair made of snakes; deadly gaze

WEAKNESS: Mirrors

MOST DASTARDLY DEED: Turning people to stone

goddess ever contrived: The poor woman's hair became a tangle of serpents. So frightful was her appearance that anyone who looked upon her was petrified (turned to stone).

"The hissing snakes her foes more sure ensnare, than they did lovers once, when shining hair."

Perhaps Medusa had no desire to petrify passersby, or perhaps she was simply terrified by this new state of affairs. Whatever the reason, she fled far

from Greece, to dwell among "devious wilds, and trackless woods," where you might think no one would find her.

Nevertheless, Medusa's lair was soon cluttered up by a "wasteful havoc" of lifelike statues. What was a Medusa to do? Wild animals and hapless wanderers kept blundering by and looking upon her face.

The nonstop petrification was Minerva's fault, really, and the goddess ought to have cleaned up the mess she made. Instead, Minerva arranged for a man named Perseus to travel from Greece and kill Medusa.

Step one was helping Perseus acquire the items he would need on his mission: winged sandals, a mirror, and a sickle-sword. With his winged sandals, Perseus flew to the strange land where Medusa lived. He located her with his mirror—no eye contact, no risk. Then he crept up backward on her as she slept, and, with a backhanded "unerring blow" of his sickle-sword, chopped off her head.

Out of her neck sprang an armored warrior and a winged horse, Pegasus. Out of her blood sprang all the species of poisonous snakes.

But Medusa had the last laugh. Perseus carried her severed head around with him for years, using it to turn his enemies to stone. One day Perseus displayed Medusa's terrifying visage to an enemy general who was blind. The blind man was unaffected, of course. Puzzled by the fact that the head had failed him, Perseus turned it around to make sure it was still working, and immediately turned to stone himself.

BEYOND THE BOOK

MEDUSA'S COUSINS

Medusa isn't the only monster that can take you out with a look. There's also the basilisk. The great writer Thomas Browne, in his *Pseudodoxia Epidemica* (1646), describes the basilisk as being either a "kind of Serpent, not above three palms long" with "some white marks or coronary spots upon the crown," or a monster having "legs, wings, a Serpentine and winding tail, and a crist or comb somewhat like a Cock." The most distinctive thing about it is "that it killeth at a distance, that it poisoneth by the eye."

Medusa isn't even the only monster that can turn you to stone. The Kwakiutl people of the American Pacific Northwest speak of a two-headed snake (with a bonus human head in the middle) called Sisiutl, whose touch can petrify you.

HEROIC COUPLETS

Ovid wrote the *Metamorphoses* in Latin, but many writers over the centuries have translated his stories into English. The translation used in this chapter is from 1717, and many of the best poets of the day, including John Dryden and Joseph Addison, worked on it. For their translation, they used the most popular verse form of the day, *heroic couplets*.

Heroic couplets are pairs of rhyming lines written in iambic pentameter, meaning that each line has ten syllables and every other syllable is stressed, starting with the second one. The couplet usually makes a complete thought. Often it's just one sentence.

> *"Friends, shút your éyes," he críes: his Shíeld he tákes,*
> *And to the Kíng expósed Medúsa's Snákes.*

For a hundred years before the rise of Romanticism (see p. 114), most English poems were written this way.

MEDUSA IN SPACE!

In her science fiction story "Shambleau" (1933), Catherine L. Moore imagines a new kind of Medusa, an alien with hair made of vampiric worms that feed upon emotions. Moore speculates that the ancient myth of Medusa is based on encounters with these aliens, made by astronauts from Atlantis. "And those ancient Greeks who told the story," she writes, "must have remembered, dimly and half believing, a tale of antiquity about some strange being from one of the outlying planets their remotest ancestors once trod."

ANCIENT GREECE: LAND OF MONSTERS

You couldn't go three miles in ancient Greece or turn three pages in a book on Greek mythology without tripping over a monster. There's Medusa, of course, and Polyphemus (see p. 128) and dragons (see p. 45), as well as:

- **Hecatoncheires,** giants with a hundred hands and fifty heads (!) who fought alongside the gods in their war to overthrow the Titans.

- **The Chimera,** "who breathed raging fire, a creature fearful, great, swift-footed and strong, who had three heads, one of a grim-eyed lion; in her hinderpart, a dragon; and in her middle, a goat, breathing forth a fearful blast of blazing fire" (from Hesiod's *Theogony*, ca. 700 BC).

- **Harpies,** birds with the heads of women, who tormented King Phineus in this way: Every time he tried to eat anything, the harpies would fly by and literally poop all over it.

POLYPHEMUS

FROM

THE ODYSSEY

BY HOMER (CA. 775 BC)

Ancient Greece was a land of monsters. In Thebes there was the sphinx; in Crete there was the Minotaur; and the island of Sicily teemed with Cyclopes (*Cyclopes* is the plural of *Cyclops*), giants with one eye in the middle of their foreheads. These "lawless and inhuman" monsters herded sheep and goats and lived in caves. They were too savage to build ships, so they survived on mutton and cheese (from the goats) and the occasional shipwrecked sailor.

"Mightiest amongst all the Cyclopes" was "godlike Polyphemus," son of the sea god, Poseidon. In truth, though, he was just another "cruel wretch" who lived in a filthy cave with sheep dung "scattered in great heaps."

CATEGORY: Giant

BASE OF OPERATIONS: Sicily

WHEN: Right after the Trojan War

POWERS: He's "ever so much stronger" than the gods

WEAKNESS: Depth perception

MOST DASTARDLY DEED: Eating people

FEAR FACTOR: 💀💀💀

BATRACHOMYOMACHIA

The ancients said that Homer, after producing the two greatest epics ever written, the *Odyssey* and the *Iliad*, turned his hand to a sillier work: the *Batrachomyomachia*, or *The Battle of the Frogs and Mice* (fourth century BC). This short parody tells of an absurd war that breaks out between the tiny creatures. Critics no longer think Homer wrote this poem, but it's still the best poem we have about interspecies combat. Spoiler: The mice almost defeat the frogs, until their allies, the crabs, come as reinforcements. Crabs have both natural weapons and natural armor!

One day, Polyphemus had the misfortune to encounter the cunning sailor Odysseus, who was sailing back home from Troy with a boatload of his men. Odysseus had landed on the island to learn if the Cyclopes were "uncivilized savages, or a hospitable and humane race." It turned out they were the former.

When Odysseus and his men met Polyphemus, Odysseus asked to be welcomed as a guest. And what did Polyphemus do? He grabbed two of Odysseus's men, bashed their heads on the floor of the cave, "tore them limb from limb," and "gobbled them up like a lion in the wilderness, flesh, bones, marrow, and entrails, without leaving anything uneaten."

Then Polyphemus blocked the entrance to his cave with a boulder "so huge that two and twenty strong four-wheeled wagons would not be enough to draw it from its place," and lay down to sleep. Nearby slept his flocks of enormous sheep and goats, and near them, listening to the giant's dreadful snores, trembled Odysseus and his surviving men, their hearts "broken for terror."

So passed the night.

In the morning, Polyphemus breakfasted on two more men and then rolled away the great boulder just long enough to shoo his flocks through and slip outside himself. He rolled it back again and spent the day happily roaming the fields and basking in the sun.

In the dark, wretched cave, Odysseus plotted.

Now Odysseus was the cleverest of men, "that ingenious hero," "that man, so ready at need." He always had a trick up his sleeve.

He put his men to work there in the cave. The giant had left behind his staff, a trunk the size of "the mast of a twenty-oared merchant vessel," and Odysseus had a six-foot piece sliced off. His men sharpened it to a point, hardening the point in the fire, and hid it under a pile of dung.

Polyphemus brought his flocks back to the cave at night and supped on two more men. Odysseus said to him,

"You have been eating a great deal of man's flesh."

Pointing out that Polyphemus must be thirsty, he offered the Cyclops some wine. Polyphemus thanked him and promised to kill him last. He asked Odysseus for his name.

"Noman," lied Odysseus.

Soon Polyphemus was sleeping deeply, and Odysseus and his men dug out their filthy spear. They heated it in the fire until it was smoldering, and then plunged the hot point right into the Cyclops's one eye "till the boiling blood bubbled all over it," "so that the steam from the burning eyeball scalded his eyelids and eyebrows, and the roots of the eye sputtered in the fire."

Polyphemus, waking, screamed through the wall of the cave:

"NOMAN IS SLAYING ME!"

And the other Cyclopes, hearing this, wondered why Polyphemus was shouting about something so uninteresting. After all, no man was slaying them as well. Needless to say, they did not come to help.

The next day, Polyphemus let his flocks out again, but this time he sat in the cave entrance to make sure no men slipped through. But Odysseus and his men were one step ahead of him and rode out of the cave clinging to the wool on the underbellies of the giant sheep. They drove the animals to their ship and sailed away, having stolen not only Polyphemus's eye, but also his flock.

But as he sailed away, Odysseus made his big mistake: He shouted his real name to the raging blind Cyclops. Polyphemus begged his father, Poseidon, to set a vengeful sea against Odysseus and his men.

Poseidon did his work well. It would take Odysseus ten years to get home, and all his men died along the way. Thus was Polyphemus avenged.

SINBAD AND THE ADVENTURE OF THE VERY SAME STORY

In some versions of the story collection *One Thousand and One Nights* (ca. thirteenth century), Sinbad the Sailor has several adventures that closely resemble parts of the *Odyssey*. On his third voyage, for example, Sinbad and his men encounter a giant with one eye "like a burning coal in the middle of his forehead." The giant eats people until he falls asleep, whereupon Sinbad and eight others blind the giant with "a spit" "made red-hot in the fire." It all sounds so familiar . . .

BEYOND THE BOOK

HOMER'S BLOOMING LYRE

Rudyard Kipling, author of *The Jungle Book* (1894), wrote about Homer in *The Seven Seas* (1896):

> When 'Omer smote 'is bloomin' lyre,
>   He'd 'eard men sing by land an' sea;
> An' what he thought 'e might require,
>   'E went an' took—the same as me!

Kipling doesn't mean that Homer was a shoplifter. He means that Homer's stories are all old stories, and he borrowed his plots from older storytellers—just as Kipling and countless other writers have.

> They knew 'e stole; 'e knew they knowed.
>   They didn't tell, nor make a fuss,
> But winked at 'Omer down the road,
>   An' 'e winked back—the same as us!

OTHER LITERARY GIANTS

Folklore and legend are filled with ferocious giants (case in point: "Jack and the Beanstalk"), but writers have also found giants useful for—of all things—philosophical satires.

- *Gargantua* by François Rabelais (1534). This novel was published before people had a good idea of what novels should look like, so it's much weirder than most books you'll read. It is both a philosophical work and a collection of toilet jokes. The main character, the giant Gargantua, is the source of our word *gargantuan*.

- **Gulliver's Travels** by Jonathan Swift (1726). On Gulliver's first voyage, he visits Lilliput, the land of tiny people, but his second voyage is to Brobdingnag, a land of giants. Although the Brobdingnagians have (as befits their size) great hearts and are wise and reasonable when compared to humans, Gulliver is obsessed with how disgusting the human body is when seen at such proportions. The giants' skin, when viewed up close, is "so varied with spots, pimples, and freckles, that nothing could appear more nauseous," and it emits a "very offensive smell."

- **Micromégas** by Voltaire (1752). Micromégas is a giant from a planet "21,600,000 times greater in circumference than our little Earth" who tours the Milky Way. He stops at Saturn, which "is hardly nine times bigger than Earth, and the citizens of this country are dwarfs"—dwarfs in Micromégas's eyes, that is, for each Saturnian "is only 6,000 feet tall." When Micromégas gets to Earth, he runs into trouble because his microscope can't pick up anything smaller than a whale.

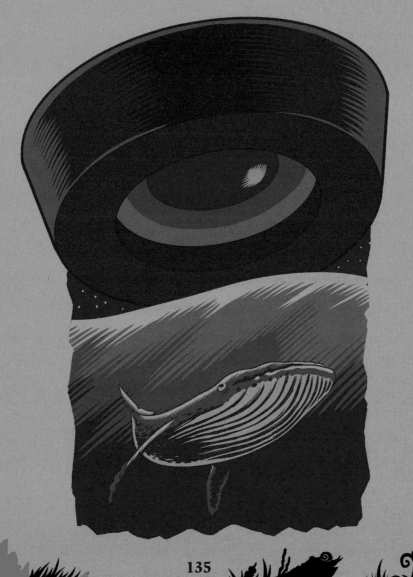

RAKSHASI

FROM

FOLK-TALES OF BENGAL

BY LAL BEHARI DAY (1883)

One day in ancient Bengal, a young man named Champa Dal came across "a magnificent palace" that appeared to be completely empty. He wandered through the rooms, "but though they were all richly furnished he did not see a single human being." Tucked away in one nook, though, was the corpse of a princess lying next to two scepters, one of silver and one of gold. When Champa Dal tapped the princess with the silver scepter . . . nothing happened. When he tapped her with the gold, though, the dead woman awoke!

She told him her name was Keshavati, and that he was in terrible danger, for the palace was surrounded by "no less than seven hundred Rakshasas."

CATEGORY: **Giant**

BASE OF OPERATIONS:
Bengal, India

WHEN: **A long time ago**

POWERS: **Shape-shifting**

MOST DASTARDLY DEED:
**"Depopulating" whole regions
(by eating everyone in sight)**

FEAR FACTOR: 💀 💀 💀 💀

Rakshasas and Rakshasis—a Rakshasa was male, a Rakshasi female—were "huge giants and giantesses, or rather demons" that plagued Bengal. "The word means literally raw-eaters," and these giants craved raw flesh, especially the raw flesh of humans.

Every morning, the giants would leave the palace in search of food and not come home until evening. They had already eaten the former king (Keshavati's father), as well as her whole family, the royal court, and every human who lived nearby.

They were unstoppable—not only were there seven hundred of them, but not one of them could be killed. Swords, arrows, elephant tusks: Everything just bounced off them harmlessly, for they hid their souls someplace secret, far away from their bodies. They were "practically immortal."

Princess Keshavati was the only human for miles around, and she was only still there because one particular aged Rakshasi had taken a shine to her and kept her as a servant. Every morning before she left to go eat people, the Rakshasi tapped Keshavati with the silver scepter, killing her. Then, in the evening, she tapped her with the gold scepter and brought her back to life.

Champa Dal thought this sounded like a very unpleasant lot to endure, but he had little time to dwell on that, because it was almost evening and soon seven hundred Rakshasas would be returning. So Champa Dal killed Keshavati with the silver scepter and hid himself in a nearby temple.

Sure enough, just then seven hundred Rakshasas returned from their "hunting and predatory excursions." The old Rakshasi came to Princess

Keshavati's room, brought her to life with the gold scepter, and said: "Hye, mye, khye! A human being I smell."

Keshavati persuaded the monster that she only smelled her, the princess. This seemed to appease the Rakshasi, who flopped down "her huge body, which looked like a part of the Himalaya mountains," and soon fell asleep. In the morning, she killed Princess Keshavati and left again.

When Champa Dal emerged from hiding that day, he brought the princess back to life and the two of them cooked up a plan. That evening, he killed her again and returned to the temple.

In came the old Rakshasi, and after tapping the princess with the gold scepter, she said once more: "Hye, mye, khye! A human being I smell."

But Princess Keshavati distracted the old Rakshasi with tears. She pretended that she was worried, for her mistress was so very old, and soon she might die, and the other Rakshasas would eat her body raw.

The Rakshasi just laughed and told Keshavati not to worry. She said that her life, and the lives of the other seven hundred Raksahasas, were guarded by "a secret which no human being can unravel."

There was a well in the palace, she explained, and at the bottom of that well was a crystal pillar, and on the crystal pillar lived two bees. If anyone ever managed to dive into the water, swim to the pillar, seize the bees, bring them to the surface, "and destroy them so that not a drop of their blood falls to the ground" (for "if a single drop of blood falls to the ground, then from it will start up a thousand Rakshasas")—if anyone were to do all that, then sure, all the Rakshasas would die. But

what were the odds of anyone pulling off such a feat? The Rakshasas were perfectly safe. Then the Rakshasi went to sleep, and in the morning, she killed the princess and left.

So Champa Dal brought the princess back to life, and she told him the secret.

Right away, Champa Dal found the well, placed a knife and a pile of ashes beside it, and dived in. When he came out, bees in hand, he picked up the knife and chopped off their little heads over the ash pile. Their bee blood "fell, not on the ground, but on the ashes."

And at that very moment, "the bees were killed, all the Rakshasas died, and their carcasses fell on the very spot on which they were standing." One huge Rakshasa corpse blocked the door of the palace, and Champa Dal and Princess Keshavati had to climb through a window to get out.

Of course, Champa Dal and Keshavati got married, and they had many adventures over many years, most of them involving hungry Rakshasis.

BEYOND THE BOOK

COLLECTING FOLKLORE

Lal Behari Day was a writer and editor in India when it was part of the British Empire (despite the efforts of Captain Nemo—see p. 22). A native of the Bengal region, he became famous for a novel he wrote in English about Bengali life. Day was the only Bengali writer many British people had ever read.

One British soldier wrote to Day asking if he could also produce "a collection of those unwritten stories which old women in India recite to little children in the evenings." Day had read *Grimm's Fairy Tales* (1812) and similar collections from other lands, and he thought he could do the same thing for Bengal. He traveled around the area collecting folktales from peasants, which he then translated into English.

The nineteenth century was a golden age of folklore collections. Anthropologists traveled the world, recording and publishing local folklore. Lal Behari Day was one of the very few outside of Europe to collect the folktales of his own people.

THE STENCH OF MEN

The Rakshasi's cry of "Hye, mye, khye!" might remind you of a similar line from the English fairy tale "Jack and the Beanstalk." The giant, smelling Jack, says:

Fe, Fi, Fo, Fum!
I smell the blood of an Englishman.
Be he alive or be he dead,
I'll grind his bones to make my bread.

Apparently, monsters like to shout things when they get a whiff of humanity's stench. In Lafcadio Hearn's translation of the Japanese "Goblin Spider" story (see p. 56), "a goblin, having but half a body and one eye," enters a room in which a man is hiding and says, "Hitokusai!" Hearn translates this word as: "There is the smell of a man."

THE WEIRD SISTERS

FROM

MACBETH

BY WILLIAM SHAKESPEARE (1606)

In the wild moors of Scotland lived three sisters "so withered and so wild in their attire" that they didn't even look "like the inhabitants of the earth." But there they were.

They had their little hobbies, like killing other people's pigs or turning into "a rat without a tail." They had their pets, like a cat named Graymalkin, a toad named Paddock, and a bird named Harpier. If one of them needed help, the others were quick to assist; for example, if one wanted to fly to Syria "in a sieve" to get revenge on a sailor because his wife wouldn't share her chestnuts(!), the other two would aid her by conjuring up a tailwind.

CATEGORY: Witches

BASE OF OPERATIONS: Scotland

WHEN: The 11th century

POWERS: Seeing the future, appearing and disappearing at will

MOST DASTARDLY DEED: "A deed without a name"

FEAR FACTOR: 💀💀💀💀💀

Every once in a while, all three would get together. When? "In thunder, lightning, or in rain." And one "foul and fair" day, as it thundered, they were dancing "hand in hand" when a man named Macbeth showed up.

Macbeth was the Thane (kind of like a baron) of Glamis. But when the Weird Sisters saw him, they hailed him as Thane of Glamis *and* Thane of Cawdor, who "shalt be King hereafter."

Macbeth corrected them. He was Thane of Glamis, yes, but not Thane of Cawdor, and he was not really in line to be king—so what were they talking about? But the sisters just disappeared.

Macbeth might have forgotten all about the strange experience, except just then, two messengers rode up and told Macbeth that the Thane of Cawdor had been proven traitor, and Macbeth would be the new Thane of Cawdor. Macbeth welcomed the news, and it got him thinking. Maybe he *would* be king someday. . . . After all, the witches' prophecy had already partly come true.

Meanwhile, the Weird Sisters kept taking care of witch business. They visited their evil queen, Hecate (the Greek goddess of witchcraft). They

cobbled together a disgusting witches' brew. They perpetrated "a deed without a name," whatever that is—and it doesn't sound good. Then one of them said:

"By the pricking of my thumbs, something wicked this way comes. Open, locks, whoever knocks!"

It was Macbeth, and he had some news: He had murdered the king and usurped the throne, fulfilling the witches' prophecy. And now he was worried he might not get away with it.

The Sisters conjured up three apparitions—"an armed head," "a bloody child," and "a child crowned"—who told Macbeth not to worry. They said, "none of woman born shall harm Macbeth," which was comforting. They said, "Macbeth shall never vanquished be until Great Birnam Wood to high Dunsinane Hill shall come against him," which was even better. Birnam Wood and Dunsinane Hill were nowhere near each other, and forests don't just march across the country to a hill! And who was not "of woman born"?

The Sisters did a little dance and disappeared again, and that was the last they were seen.

Macbeth, of course, met a bad end. The army that marched against him came bearing boughs from Birnam Wood, and in this way, Birnam Wood did indeed come to Dunsinane. A man named Macduff, who faced off against Macbeth in single combat, "was from his mother's womb untimely ripped"—that is, he was delivered by a C-section—and therefore was not technically "of woman born."

The sisters' words had come true. Macduff cut off Macbeth's head.

BEYOND THE BOOK

WHY ARE THERE WITCHES HERE ANYWAY?

William Shakespeare based most of his plays on older stories, and *Macbeth* is based on a real eleventh-century Scottish king, whose life story is told in the not-very-accurate history book *Holinshed's Chronicles* (1577).

Holished's Chronicles doesn't have witches in it, though. Instead, Macbeth meets "nymphs or feiries" living in the woods, and they give him the misleading prophesies. So why did Shakespeare change the "feiries" into witches?

When Shakespeare was writing *Macbeth*, he knew King James I would be in the play's audience—and King James was obsessed with witches. His fiancée (Princess Anne of Denmark) had encountered rough weather when sailing to Britain, and some Danish witches confessed under torture to conjuring up the storms. That was enough for James, who started seeing witches everywhere. Shakespeare knew that adding witches to his play would keep the king interested.

BABA YAGA

Alexander Afanasyev collected Russian fairy tales and published them in many volumes between 1855 and 1863. Several of the stories feature a witch named Baba Yaga. She lives in a hut that walks on chicken legs, surrounded by "twelve poles in a circle, and on each of eleven of these poles" is "stuck a human head." (The twelfth is reserved for her next visitor.) Baba Yaga eats "up men as though they were poultry," and she can fly through the air "in her iron mortar, urging it on with the pestle, sweeping away her traces with the broom."

WHAT'S FOR SUPPER?

The Weird Sisters are witches, and witches will have their brew. The most famous ingredients in their cauldron are "eye of newt and toe of frog, wool of bat and tongue of dog," but there are many others, equally gross:

- an adder's "fork" (forked tongue)

- a lizard's leg

- a mummified witch

- the esophagus and stomach of a shark

- a dragon's scale

- baboon's blood

- the sweat of a hanged murderer

- the blood of a sow who has eaten all her piglets(!)

- the finger of a baby strangled at birth(!!)

- a hemlock root

That last one doesn't sound so bad, but the philosopher Socrates drank hemlock once and it killed him. At least baboon's blood isn't poisonous.

WITCHES REDEEMED!

In the old witch-hunting days of Cotton Mather and James I, witches were always evil, but their image has softened over the centuries. In L. Frank Baum's *The Wonderful Wizard of Oz* (1900), 50 percent of Oz's witches are good (and 50 percent are evil). In J. K. Rowling's Harry Potter books, the word *witch* is just a feminine form of *wizard*, and only a few Slytherins are actually wicked.

WHITE FELL

FROM

THE WERE-WOLF

BY CLEMENCE HOUSMAN (1896)

In the old and savage days, a woman called White Fell wandered the wilds of medieval Europe, living a "bold free huntress life." Her eyes were as "blue as the sky" and "her hair fair, and in plaits to the waist." Wherever she went, she wore white furs (*fell* is an old word meaning "fur"), and carried a small double-headed ax in her belt. Oh, and she was a werewolf.

During the day, she could change freely from human form to wolf form and back again, but at the stroke of midnight, she always had to change into a wolf, and should anyone ever see her change, she could never become human again.

CATEGORY: Lycanthrope

BASE OF OPERATIONS: Northern Europe

WHEN: Long ago

POWERS: Superspeed and superstrength; skilled with an ax; she can TURN INTO A WOLF

WEAKNESS: Holy water

MOST DASTARDLY DEED: Eating a toddler

FEAR FACTOR: 💀💀💀💀

One winter day, White Fell padded on wolf feet to a rustic "farm hall," reassuming her human form to seek shelter. The great hall housed a whole village's worth of people during the long winter months, and they welcomed the stranger. She told "strange tales of fierce attack and defense" and charmed everyone with her beauty and her warmth. Little Rol, a boy about three years old, climbed on her lap and she gave him a kiss that felt "like a snowflake." Only the dog didn't like her; he kept growling and had to be chained in a corner.

Especially charmed by White Fell's grace and beauty was a great warrior named Sweyn. Sweyn's twin brother, Christian, noticed that the tracks White Fell made leading to the hall were wolf tracks and tried to warn his brother: She's a werewolf! But Sweyn laughed it off. Only doddering old women like old Trella believed in werewolves. They'd say that the way to kill a werewolf was to "sprinkle hands and feet with holy water."

During the night, White Fell slipped away from the hall through an open window. Days later, little Rol went missing.

In January, White Fell returned to the hall when Christian was away. She and Sweyn exchanged stories of brave deeds and dangers, and White Fell sang a beautiful, mournful song:

Far up the plain
Moans on a voice of pain:
"Where shall my babe be lain?"

Old Trella was moved to tears by the song, which reminded her of her own children, long dead. White Fell kissed her, and then she abruptly left just as Christian came home. "God help us all! She is a Were-Wolf," Christian said, but everyone said Christian was just plain crazy.

Then old Trella disappeared without a trace.

Sweyn was still smitten. He courted White Fell, and one day she gave him a kiss. It was the kiss of death, Christian knew. White Fell had eaten Rol and Trella, and now she was going to eat Sweyn, too. This time, when White Fell left the hall, Christian followed her across the snow.

"Fell Thing," he called her, for *fell* is also an old word meaning "wicked and deadly." And she gave him "a beastly snarl, teeth and eyes gleaming."

Christian had a spear, but White Fell chopped it in two with her ax. Then she hacked him up until he fell. She turned into a wolf and jumped on his

WEREWOLVES VS. VAMPIRES

In the 1884 historical novel *With Fire and Sword* by Henryk Sienkiewicz, a boy asks his father whether werewolves or vampires are the strongest. The father replies:

The werewolf is stronger, but the vampire is more stubborn. If you are able to get the upper hand of the werewolf, he will serve you, but vampires are good for nothing except to follow blood. The werewolf is always ataman [leader] over the vampires.

body, ready to finish him off—but this was her undoing. For "no holy water could be more holy, more potent to destroy an evil thing than the life-blood of a pure heart." All four feet landed in Christian's blood, and the wolf keeled over dead.

So fell White Fell, who only wanted to eat the occasional unsuspecting villager. When Sweyn found the two corpses frozen next to each other, he had no choice but to admit that his brother was right.

His girlfriend had been a werewolf.

"I FEAR NEITHER MAN NOR BEAST; SOME FEW FEAR ME."
—WHITE FELL

BEYOND THE BOOK

OTHER LITERARY WEREWOLVES

Two thousand years before *Twilight*, werewolves were already sneaking around books.

- ***The Satyricon*** by Petronius (ca. 60). The first werewolf in all of literature comes from this two-thousand-year-old Latin novel, one of the first novels ever written. A traveler takes off his clothes and urinates in a circle around them; suddenly the clothes turn into rocks and the traveler turns into a wolf. No later werewolf book includes that bit about the rocks . . .

- ***The Wolf-Leader*** by Alexandre Dumas (1857). Dumas is best remembered for his novels *The Three Musketeers* (1844) and *The Count of Monte Cristo* (1844), but this prolific writer cranked out more than fifty other books in his lifetime—including one werewolf novel about a poor cobbler who makes a deal with a talking wolf: The cobbler gets his wishes granted, but in return he slowly transforms into a werewolf.

- **"Gabriel-Ernest"** by Saki (1910). H. H. Munro wrote morbid, humorous stories under the pen name "Saki." Few are as morbid as this tale of a sixteen-year-old werewolf who eats, as he puts it, "rabbits, wild-fowl, hares, poultry, lambs in their season, children when I can get any; they're usually too well locked in at night, when I do most of my hunting. It's quite two months since I tasted child-flesh."

WEREWOLF RULES

In Sabine Baring-Gould's 1865 study, *The Book of Were-Wolves*, we learn that you can identify a werewolf in human form "by the meeting of his eyebrows above the nose," that they "are obliged at each full moon to transform themselves" into wolf form, and that "if the were-wolf be thrice addressed by his baptismal name, he resumes his human form."

We now know that werewolves can be killed with a silver bullet, but Baring-Gould never mentions this. Perhaps it's a more recent discovery?

ZAHHAK

FROM
THE SHAHNAMEH
BY FERDOWSI (1010)

It starts like a fairy tale: A long time ago, in the land of Arabia, the lived a prince named Zahhak.

One day, a man called Eblis approached the crown prince Zahhak and whispered in his ear that he would be a better king than his fathe For the good of the country, Eblis said, the better king must be put on the throne . . . which meant that the old king, alas, had to die.

So, with some regret, Zahhak and Eblis plotted the king's murder. They dug a pit in the king's garden, and on an afternoon stroll, the king fell in and broke his neck. Quick work with the shovel buried all evidence of the crime.

CATEGORY: Cursed human

BASE OF OPERATIONS: Persia, and most of the world

WHEN: An awful long time ago

POWERS: Snakes for shoulders

MOST DASTARDLY DEED:

Soon Zahhak was king of Arabia and everyone was happy. But Eblis suggested to his friend King Zahhak that he could have even more. Why be content as king of Arabia when he could be king of the world?

As Zahhak mulled over this advice, Eblis secretly kissed the king on his shoulders. From each shoulder sprang a snake, hissing and spitting right next to Zahhak's ears. The king cut the snakes from his shoulders with a knife, but they simply grew back again "like branches from a tree."

Night and day, the snakes writhed, for they were hungry. They were driving Zahhak crazy! Eblis, as chief advisor, suggested that the best way to get rid of the snakes would be to feed them daily on the brains of two men. Such a diet would surely kill the snakes. So Zahhak had two of his subjects slain every day and fed their brains to his shoulder snakes. But the snakes did not sicken and die as he hoped. They grew stronger. Zahhak grew stronger, too, and people began to call him the Dragon King.

Not content with just being king of Arabia, Zahhak assembled an army and marched into neighboring Persia. The rightful king of Persia, Jamshyd, had been reigning for seven hundred years, but Zahhak pursued him to the ends of the earth and cut him in two with a saw.

Persia was the most important kingdom in the world at the time, and Zahhak found that, in becoming king of Persia, he had "slipped on the world as 'twere a finger-ring."

After that things got bad.

Believe it or not, a king with man-eating snakes growing out of his shoulders was not the best choice to rule the world. For a thousand years Zahhak reigned, encouraging every evil deed. Slavery, necromancy, and arson flourished. For a thousand years, "no man spake of good unless by stealth." And of course, every day, another two men died and their brains went to the snakes. Every day for a thousand years.

One day, Zahhak gathered all the sages and wisest men in the world to his court, and he asked them to sign a document proclaiming that everything Zahhak had ever done had been for the greater good, that he "speaketh truth and wrongeth none." The terrified sages were in the process of signing when a blacksmith named Kaveh stormed into the castle, demanding justice.

"Tell us who hath wronged thee," Zahhak said.

Kaveh said that it was Zahhak who had wronged him. His son had just been taken to provide snake food, and this, Kaveh insisted, was an injustice.

Surprised by the public rebuke, Zahhak released the son and asked Kaveh to sign the proclamation. But Kaveh was not satisfied, and after reading the

document, he tore it in two and trampled the pieces. Then he went outside and began calling in the marketplace for the end of Zahhak's reign. He hung his leather smith's apron on a spear as a rallying flag. Wherever he went, people flocked to his banner, for they had come to hate Zahhak and his evil ways.

Now, although Zahhak had long ago tried to kill all of King Jamshyd's relatives, one grandnephew named Feraydun still lived. When Feraydun heard of Kaveh, he assembled an army, joined forces with the blacksmith, and took the leather apron as his own battle standard.

Feraydun marched on Zahhak's palace and Zahhak fled in fear before the might of his army . . . only to slip back in by secret ways to kill Feraydun a day later. But Feraydun saw the Dragon King and struck him with a mace the size of "a mountain crag," with the image of an ox's head carved on top. One blow from such a weapon knocked Zahhak senseless.

Feraydun did not kill Zahhak, but he bound him with a lasso and then nailed him down upon a rock in a narrow gorge in Mount Damavand. There, Zahhak stayed, "so his anguish might endure."

He may be there still, but maybe not. After all, the snakes on his shoulders have only one brain to feast on now . . .

BEYOND THE BOOK

THE REST OF THE *SHAHNAMEH* (ABRIDGED)

The story of Zahhak comes from the *Shahnameh*, or the "Book of Kings," an epic Persian poem written by Ferdowsi a thousand years ago. Much of the poem is concerned with the great deeds of monster-fighting heroes, especially Rustum, a Hercules-like warrior who rides an enormous horse and fights with a great club. Rustum battles lions and invisible dragons and evil hags—and also other great warriors, such as Esfandiyar, a man who can only be killed by a shot through both eyes with a double-headed arrow. Rustum, of course, makes the shot.

Ferdowsi's poem continues into historical times, including Alexander the Great's conquest of Persia and the wars of Persia and Rome, and concludes with the Muslim Arabs' invasion of Persia in the seventh century—an event that marked the end of traditional Persian culture.

SOHRAB AND RUSTUM

One part of the *Shahnameh* is best known to English speakers from an adaptation by the poet Matthew Arnold. His long poem "Sohrab and Rustum" (1853) tells the story of the Persian hero Rustum, who fights his son in combat without recognizing him. Only after stabbing his enemy with a spear does Rustum realize he has killed his own son.

> He cast
> His arms round his son's neck, and wept aloud,
> And kiss'd him. And awe fell on both the hosts,
> When they saw Rustum's grief . . .

All of Matthew Arnold's great poems are depressing. His most famous poem, "Dover Beach" (1867), is all about how life is meaningless and possesses "neither joy, nor love, nor light, / Nor certitude, nor peace, nor help for pain." A grieving Rustum might agree.

ALL THE BOOKS MENTIONED IN THIS BOOK

All of these books are old enough to be in the public domain, which means they are free to copy and distribute, and you can easily find them on the internet on Archive.org, Project Gutenberg, or Google Books. (Not all translations are public domain though, and some books have no English translations old enough.)

While all these books are well worth a read, the books in purple are the most fun and accessible, so it might be best to start with those. The books in **bold** are the sources for the twenty-five monsters featured in this book.

THE BOOKS

Alexander Afanasyev, *Russian Fairy Tales* (1915)

Ogita Ansei, *Tonoigusa* (1660)

Apollodorus, *Library* (ca. the 2nd century)

Apollonius of Rhodes, *Argonautica* (ca. 250 BC)

Ludovico Ariosto, *Cinque Canti* (1545)

Ludovico Ariosto, *Orlando Furioso* (1532)

Matthew Arnold, "Dover Beach" (1867)

Matthew Arnold, "Sohrab and Rustum" (1853)

Jane Austen, *Northanger Abbey* (1818)

Sabine Baring-Gould, *The Book of Were-Wolves* (1865)

Sabine Baring-Gould, "Margery of Quether" (1884)

Bartholomeus Anglicus, *On the Properties of Things* (1240)

The Battle of the Frogs and Mice (4th century BC)

L. Frank Baum, *The Wonderful Wizard of Oz* (1900)

E. F. Benson, "The Room in the Tower" (1912)

Beowulf (ca. 750)

Algernon Blackwood, "The Wendigo" (1910)

Mary Elizabeth Braddon, "Good Lady Ducayne" (1896)

Thomas Browne, *Pseudodoxia Epidemica* (1646)

E. A. Wallis Budge, ed., *The Babylonian Legends of the Creation and the Fight Between Bel and the Dragon* (1921)

E. A. Wallis Budge, ed., *The Book of the Dead* (1895)

E. A. Wallis Budge, ed., *The Chapters of Coming Forth by Day* (1898)

E. A. Wallis Budge, ed., *The Egyptian Heaven and Hell* (1905)

Thomas Bulfinch, *Legends of Charlemagne* (1864)

Thomas Bulfinch, *Age of Fable* (1855)

Edgar Rice Burroughs, *A Princess of Mars* (1912)

Karel Čapek, *R.U.R.* (1921)

Lewis Carroll, *Alice's Adventures in Wonderland* (1865)

Lewis Carroll, *The Hunting of the Snark* (1876)

Lewis Carroll, "Phantasmagoria" (1869)

Lewis Carroll, *Through the Looking-Glass* (1871)

Robert W. Chambers, *The Maker of Moons* (1896)

Samuel Taylor Coleridge, *Christabel* (1816)

Carlo Collodi, *The Adventures of Pinocchio* (1883)

Padraic Colum, *The Children of Odin* (1920)

Walter Crane, *Valentine and Orson* (1870)

F. Marion Crawford, "For the Blood Is the Life" (1911)

Cynaethus of Chios, *Hymn to Apollo* (ca. 522 BC)

Lal Behari Day, *Folk-Tales of Bengal* (1883)

Charles Dickens, *A Christmas Carol* (1843)

Arthur Conan Doyle, "Lot No. 249" (1892)

Alexandre Dumas, *The Count of Monte Cristo* (1844)

Alexandre Dumas, *The Three Musketeers* (1844)

Alexandre Dumas, *The Wolf Leader* (1857)

Epic of Gilgamesh (ca. 1750 BC)

Ferdowsi, *Shahnameh* (ca. 1010)

Edward FitzGerald, *Rubáiyát of Omar Khayyám* (1859–1889)

Elizabeth Gaskell, "Clopton House" (1838)

Théophile Gautier, "The Mummy's Foot" (1840)

J. W. von Goethe, *The Sorrows of Young Werther* (1774)

Robert Greene, *Friar Bacon and Friar Bungay* (ca. 1590)

Jacob and Wilhelm Grimm, *Grimms' Fairy Tales* (1812)

W. S. Harris, *Life in a Thousand Worlds* (1905)

Nathaniel Hawthorne, "Rappaccini's Daughter" (1844)

Lafcadio Hearn, "In a Japanese Garden" (1892)

Lafcadio Hearn, *Japanese Fairy Tales* (Second Series No. 1) (1899)

Lafcadio Hearn, *Kwaidan* (1904)

Hesiod, *Theogony* (ca. 700 BC)

Raphael Holinshed, et al., *Holinshed's Chronicles* (1577)

Homer, The Iliad (ca. 760 BC)

Homer, *The Odyssey* (ca. 775 BC)

Clemence Housman, *The Were-Wolf* (1896)

Victor Hugo, *The Hunchback of Notre-Dame* (1831)

Victor Hugo, *Toilers of the Sea* (1866)

Washington Irving, "The Legend of Sleepy Hollow" (1820)

Henry James, *The Turn of the Screw* (1898)

M. R. James, "'Oh, Whistle and I'll Come to You, My Lad'" (1904)

Franz Kafka, *The Metamorphosis* (1915)

John Keats, "La Belle Dame sans Merci" (1819)

John Keats, *Lamia* (1820)

Rudyard Kipling, The Jungle Books (1894–1895)

Rudyard Kipling, *Just So Stories* (1902)

Rudyard Kipling, *The Seven Seas* (1896)

Joseph Sheridan Le Fanu, *Carmilla* (1872)

Gaston Leroux, *The Phantom of the Opera* (1910)

Jack London, "The Shadow and the Flash" (1903)

H. P. Lovecraft, "The Call of Cthulhu" (1928)

H. P. Lovecraft, "Supernatural Horror in Literature" (1927)

Lucian, *A True Story* (ca. 150)

Charles Mackay, *Lost Beauties of the English Language* (1874)

John Mandeville, *The Travels of Sir John Mandeville* (1357)

Gaston Maspero, ed., *Popular Stories of Ancient Egypt* (1882)

Cotton Mather, *The Wonders of the Invisible World* (1693)

Guy de Maupassant, "The Horla" (1887)

Gustav Meyrink, *The Golem* (1915)

Thomas Middleton, *The Revenger's Tragedy* (ca. 1606)

John Milton, *Paradise Lost* (1667)

C. L. Moore, "Shambleau" (1933)

William Morris, *The Story of Sigurd the Volsung and the Fall of the Niblungs* (1876)

One Thousand and One Nights (ca. 13th century)

Ovid, *The Metamorphoses* (ca. 8)

Thomas Love Peacock, *Crotchet Castle* (1831)

Thomas Love Peacock, *Nightmare Abbey* (1818)

Petronius, *Satyricon* (ca. 60)

Plato, *The Republic* (ca. 380 BC)

Plutarch, *Lives* (ca. 100)

Edgar Allan Poe, "The Fall of the House of Usher" (1839)

Edgar Allan Poe, "Some Words with a Mummy" (1845)

John William Polidori, *The Vampyre* (1819)

François Rabelais, *Gargantua* (1534)

Ann Radcliffe, *The Mysteries of Udolpho* (1794)

Knud Rasmussen, *Eskimo Folk-Tales* (1921)

Rustichello de Pisa, *The Travels of Marco Polo* (1298)

Saki, "Gabriel-Ernest" (1910)

William Shakespeare, *Hamlet* (ca. 1600)

William Shakespeare, *Julius Caesar* (1599)

William Shakespeare, *Macbeth* (1606)

William Shakespeare, *Richard III* (ca. 1593)

William Shakespeare, *The Tempest* (ca. 1610)

Mary Shelley, *Frankenstein* (1818)

Henryk Sienkiewicz, *With Fire and Sword* (1884)

Sophocles, *Oedipus the King* (429 BC)

Robert Louis Stevenson, *The Strange Case of Dr. Jekyll and Mr. Hyde* (1886)

Bram Stoker, *Dracula* (1897)

Jonathan Swift, *Gulliver's Travels* (1726)

Joshua Sylvester, *Birth of the World* (1592)

Alfred, Lord Tennyson, "The Kraken" (1830)

Mark Twain, *Adventures of Huckleberry Finn* (1884)

Jules Verne, *Master of the World* (1904)

Jules Verne, *Robur the Conqueror* (1886)

Jules Verne, *Twenty Thousand Leagues Under the Sea* (1870)

Jules Verne, "A Voyage in a Balloon" (1851)

The Volsung Saga (ca. 13th century)

Voltaire, *Micromégas* (1752)

The Voyage of Saint Brendan the Abbot (ca. 900)

Hugh Walpole, *The Castle of Otranto* (1764)

Jane Webb, *The Mummy!* (1827)

John Webster, *The White Devil* (1612)

H. G. Wells, *Floor Games* (1911)

H. G. Wells, *The Invisible Man* (1897)

H. G. Wells, *The Island of Dr. Moreau* (1896)

H. G. Wells, *Little Wars* (1913)

H. G. Wells, *The Time Machine* (1895)

H. G. Wells, *The War of the Worlds* (1898)

Edith Wharton, "Afterward" (1910)

Oscar Wilde, *The Ballad of Reading Gaol* (1897)

Oscar Wilde, *The Picture of Dorian Gray* (1890)

FURTHER READING

Many of the monsters and other characters featured in this book appear in a variety of stories throughout time. Here are recommendations for exploring some of these characters and tales more fully.

GOLEMS: The legend of the Golem appears in many books, but two of the best are by Isaac Bashevis Singer and Elie Wiesel (both Nobel Prize winners). Both books are titled *The Golem*.

THE SHAHNAMEH: Several characters from *The Shahnameh* appear in Edward FitzGerald's translation of the *Rubáiyát of Omar Khayyám* (1859), which was one of the most popular poems of the nineteenth century and started a craze for Persian poetry.

DRACULA: Vampires were quite the fashion a hundred years ago, and there are lots of great vampire stories to move on to after *Dracula*. In addition to the ones we recommended in the Dracula chapter, you can try the short stories "Good Lady Ducayne" by Mary Elizabeth Braddon (1896), "For the Blood Is the Life" by F. Marion Crawford (1911), and "The Room in the Tower" by E. F. Benson (1912).

THE INVISIBLE MAN: If you can't get enough of mad scientists turning invisible, Jack London wrote a story on just that topic: "The Shadow and the Flash" (1903).

LAMIA: The detail about eyes popping out comes from Daniel Ogden's book *Perseus*, which has more information about that hero than any other book ever written. If you just want to read more by John Keats, "La Belle Dame sans Merci" (1819) is both short and terrifying.

GREEK MYTHOLOGY: For generations the first book of Greek mythology to read has been Thomas Bulfinch's *The Age of Fable* (1855). There are plenty of excellent more recent books on the subject, such as Edith Hamilton's *Mythology* or (for younger readers) *D'Aulaires' Book of Greek Myths* by Ingri and Edgar d'Aulaire.

NORSE MYTHOLOGY: The Norse gods that kill Fafnir's brother have many other adventures. The myths about them have been retold many times, but Padraic Colum's *The Children of Odin* (1920) is a particularly good one that's easily available. Much more recently, Neil Gaiman's *Norse Mythology* covers the same ground.

A NOTE ON TRANSLATIONS

Many of the monsters in this book come from books that were not originally written in English. In these cases, the quotations come from public domain translations. "Public domain" means that a text can be quoted or printed freely. Because most public domain translations are old, however, they can be a mixed bag, and some of them use deliberately archaic language for "color." If you are brave enough to read the books mentioned in this book, here are some tips on translations.

O   The two translations of Homer's *Odyssey* used—Samuel Butcher and Andrew Lang's and Samuel Butler's—are perfectly readable and a lot of fun. Butler has a pet theory that Homer was a woman, and this theory colors some of his choices, but if you just want to get a good story, these work fine. For something a little looser, *The Children's Homer* by Padraic Colum (1918) is also a good choice.

O   The *Epic of Gilgamesh* offers its own set of challenges, because the early translators were dealing with incomplete, crumbling tablets and their translations tend to be fragmentary, misinformed, and unsatisfying. Our quotes have all come from public domain translations by William Muss-Arnolt and Morris Jastrow Jr., but if you want to read *Gilgamesh* (to learn if he ever does get the secret of immortality), find a more recent version—Stephen Mitchell and Herbert Mason have good ones that are easy to find. The earliest translations, because they are based on fragments, leave out big chunks of the story, and the translators often have to guess—not very accurately—what is happening in places.

O   Although there are plenty of public domain translations of the *Shahnameh*, none of them are very good. All our quotes are from the 1905 translation by Arthur George Warner and Edmond Warner—not the worst translation, but a little dull. You might want to try instead the three volumes of *Stories from the Shahnameh of Ferdowsi*, retold by Ehsan Yarshater and translated by Dick Davis, or, if you're ambitious, Dick Davis's more faithful translation, published by Viking Books as *Shahnameh: The Persian Book of Kings*.

O   Ernest J. B. Kirtlan's translation of *Beowulf* is faithful, but not so very readable. Try something more recent instead, such as Seamus Heaney's verse translation.

- Many older translations of Jules Verne's books are heavily cut and should be read with caution. Frederick Paul Walter's translation is a recent one, used in this book with permission.

- There's no public domain translation of *The Golem*, but Mike Mitchell's is the better of the two English translations available.

- Ariosto's *Cinque Canti* has no public-domain English translation. Although *Orlando Furioso* has several, readers coming to the book for the first time may find more enjoyment reading Thomas Bulfinch's long summary in his book *Legends of Charlemagne* (1864).

- The earliest stories about Valentine and Orson are in French and German, but there are plenty of English translations to choose from. Walter Crane's *Valentine and Orson* is very short, easy to read, beautifully illustrated, and public domain. More recently, Nancy Ekholm Burkert has written a good version for young readers, also titled *Valentine and Orson*.

A LIST OF TRANSLATIONS USED

Apollonius: R. C. Seaton

Bartholomew: Robert Steele

Beowulf: Ernest J. B. Kirtlan

Cynaethus: Hugh G. Evelyn-White

Gautier: Lafcadio Hearn

Gilgamesh: 1. William Muss-Arnolt;
2. Morris Jastrow Jr.

Hesiod: Hugh G. Evelyn-White

Homer: 1. Samuel Butcher and Andrew Lang;
2. Samuel Butler

Hugo (both *Toilers* and *Hunchback*): Isabel F. HapGood

Lucian: Francis Hickes

Maspero: Mrs. C. H. W. Johns

Maupassant: Unknown

The Arabian Nights: Andrew Lang

Plutarch: Aubrey Stewart and George Long

Polo: William Marsden

Sienkiewicz: Jeremiah Curtain

Sophocles: Edward H. Plumptre

Verne: Frederick Paul Walter (*Twenty Thousand Leagues*; used with permission); Anne T. Wilbur (*Voyage/Balloon*)

Volsunga Saga: William Morris and Eirikr Magnusson

Voltaire: Peter Phalen

The Voyage of Saint Brendan the Abbot: Denis O'Donoghue

EVEN MORE MONSTERS!

There are so many great monsters from great books that you might want to dedicate the rest of your life to poring over monster stories. If so, here are twenty more nightmares to meet.

o **CALIBAN** from *The Tempest* by William Shakespeare (ca. 1610): The son of a witch and the devil, and the native of Prospero's Island, Caliban is both pitiable and monstrous.

o **CALOTS** from *A Princess of Mars* by Edgar Rice Burroughs (1912): Ten-legged pony-sized Martian dogs. Their giant mouths are like frogs' but with "three rows of long, sharp tusks."

o **CHARLOTTE CLOPTON** from "Clopton House" by Elizabeth Gaskell (1838): The ghost of a young girl who was accidentally buried alive. Sealed in the tomb, she ate one of her own shoulders "in the agonies of despair and hunger." Now, with one shoulder, she haunts her ancestral home.

o **THE GHOST OF CHRISTMAS YET TO COME** from *A Christmas Carol* by Charles Dickens (1843): The final spirit to visit the miserly Ebenezer Scrooge on Christmas Eve. "Shrouded in a deep black garment" except for one "spectral hand," this ghost offered grim visions of the future.

o **JASCONIUS** from *The Voyage of Saint Brendan the Abbott* (ca. 900): A fish so gigantic that sailors mistake it for an island; it "is ever trying to make its head and tail meet, but cannot succeed, because of its great length."

o **KALIDAHS** from *The Wonderful Wizard of Oz* by L. Frank Baum (1900): "Monstrous beasts with bodies like bears and heads like tigers."

O **KOSHCHEY THE DEATHLESS** from *Russian Fairy Tales* by Alexander Afanasyev (1915): The son of Baba Yaga, Koshchey is a sorcerer who keeps his soul in an egg instead of his body. As long as the egg remains intact, Koshchey's body cannot die.

O **LACHANOPTERS** from *A True Story* by Lucian (second century): Gigantic, space-faring birds with "leaves of lettuces" instead of feathers—just one of innumerable bizarre space creatures from Lucian's book.

O **MARGERY OF QUETHER** from "Margery of Quether" by Sabine Baring-Gould (1884): A doll-sized, shriveled-up old woman who drains the blood of the living through her single, hollow tooth.

O **THE MINOTAUR** from *Lives* by Plutarch (ca. 100): "Half-man, half-bull, in twofold shape combined," the minotaur lives in the twisting corridors of a Cretan labyrinth and eats Athenians.

O **MON-GO-DIN** from *Life in a Thousand Worlds* by W. S. Harris (1905): A gigantic "man-ape" from the planet Jupiter.

O **THE PHANTOM OF THE OPERA** from *The Phantom of the Opera* by Gaston Leroux (1910): A deformed music-buff who lives in the secret passages of the opera house he himself built.

O **QUASIMODO** from *The Hunchback of Notre-Dame* by Victor Hugo (1831): A hunchbacked, one-eyed bell-ringer, grown deaf from so many years clanging bells in Notre Dame Cathedral, with a "forked chin" and one tooth "like the tusk of an elephant."

O **THE ROC** from *The Travels of Marco Polo* (1298): A giant bird "so large and strong as to seize an elephant with its talons, and to lift it into the air, from whence it lets it fall to the ground, in order that when dead it may prey upon the carcase."

O **SCIAPODS** from *The Travels of Sir John Mandeville* (1357): A race of hopping dwarves, each with a single foot "so large, that it shadoweth all the body against the sun, when they will lie and rest."

O **THE SPHINX** from *Oedipus the King* by Sophocles (429 BC): Part lion, part lady, the Sphinx of Thebes strangles anyone who cannot answer her "dark riddle."

o **TUPILAK** from *Eskimo Folk-Tales* by Knud Rasmussen (1921): A monster fashioned by a wizard out of the carcasses and bones of people and animals, all stuck together and brought to life Frankenstein-style.

o **THE WENDIGO** from *The Wendigo* by Algernon Blackwood (1910): A wild beast from the frozen Canadian north, capable of transforming humans into smaller copies of itself.

o **THE XIN** from *The Maker of Moons* by Robert W. Chambers (1896): A cross between "a sea-urchin, a spider, and the devil," the Xin is one being with a thousand bodies that crawl independently of each other.

o **YETH-HOUNDS** from *Lost Beauties of the English Language* by Charles Mackay (1874): "Hounds without heads, supposed to be animated by the spirits of children who have died without baptism."